LAURENCE HARGER
CECILE ROSSANT

Jerry

CORNELSEN
ENGLISH
LIBRARY

Cornelsen

CORNELSEN **ENGLISH** LIBRARY
Laurence Harger, Cecile Rossant · Jerry

Verlagsredaktion
Bonnie Glänzer

Umschlaggestaltung
hawemannundmosch, Konzeption und Gestaltung, Berlin

Titelbild
Bonnie Glänzer, Berlin

Illustration
Stefan Bachmann, Wiesbaden

Gestaltung & technische Umsetzung
Buchgestaltung + Berlin

Passende Arbeitsblätter und Hinweise zum Vorgehen im Unterricht
zu diesem Titel gibt es unter www.cornelsen.de/cel

www.cornelsen.de

1. Auflage, 6. Druck 2025

Alle Drucke dieser Auflage sind inhaltlich unverändert und
können im Unterricht nebeneinander verwendet werden.

© 2015 Cornelsen Schulverlage GmbH, Berlin
© 2017 Cornelsen Verlag GmbH, Mecklenburgische Str. 53, 14197 Berlin,
E-Mail: service@cornelsen.de

Druck: AZ Druck und Datentechnik GmbH, Kempten

ISBN 978-3-06-033078-2

PEFC-zertifiziert
Dieses Produkt
stammt aus
nachhaltig
bewirtschafteten
Wäldern und
kontrollierten Quellen
PEFC/04-31-2260   www.pefc.de

CONTENTS

1 Catch me if you can

The room was dark except for the blue light from the phone on the floor.

Next to the phone, there was an empty bag and some spray cans. A hand came out of the shadows and carefully
5 put each can in the bag. Red. Yellow. Black. Then two cans of chrome-coloured paint. A drawer creaked as it was opened and again as it was closed. The hand reappeared in the light. It put a white mask in the bag and then a pair of rubber gloves. Two hands slowly closed the bag.

10 "It's 1 am, Ben. It's time to leave."

"I know."

"Do you have the keys, Ben?"

"Yesss! Now ssshh! Don't say another word until we've left the house!"

15 Everybody was talking about it at school:

"Did you see it?"

"What?"

"Someone sprayed graffiti on the gym wall."

"Really?"

20 They talked about it in the canteen at lunch:

"Graffiti? What does it say?"

"I don't know. I haven't seen it yet."

And they pointed it out on their way to PE:

"Look! There it is – on the new gym building!"

25 "Wow! It's big! But it's hard to read."

"It says: 'Catch me if you can'."

"Clever. Who did it?"

"No one knows."

Mr Edwards was teaching a Year 10 Maths class. He pointed to the right-handed triangle on the board. "Before we start looking at different equations it helps to give a name to each side of a right-angled triangle. So ..."

There was a knock on the door and Mr O'Reilly, the head PE teacher came in.

"Excuse me for interrupting your lesson, John. Ben Reckord is in your class, isn't he?"

"Yes, he is."

"Good. He needs to come with me to the head teacher's office ... immediately."

Ben felt 24 pairs of eyes follow his every movement as he walked to the door.

Well, now they really have something to be excited about, Ben thought as he left the room.

Mr O'Reilly gave Ben a quick, not altogether friendly push on the shoulder as they made their way down the empty corridor. Ben tried not to be nervous, but it wasn't working. His heart was racing and he could feel the sweat on his forehead. Mr O'Reilly opened the door to the head teacher's office and gave Ben another push as if to say: 'Get in there, you little hooligan!'

Ben was met by two familiar faces: there was his mother, in her business suit, and his dad in a comfortable T-shirt and jeans, as always.

What were they doing here?

"Mum? Dad?" They didn't answer. Ben's dad looked as if he were in pain. His mother just looked angry – really angry.

"Hello, Ben. Come over here, please, and sit down," said Mrs Taylor, the head teacher. She pointed to an empty chair next to his mother. "I'd like you to watch something. Mr O'Reilly, can you please turn off the lights."

And there they sat in the dark. Mrs Taylor turned her computer screen towards the small audience. In the front
5 row were Ben, his Mum and Dad. Mr O'Reilly was behind them. Everybody called him 'Eagle' because his sharp grey eyes seemed to catch every crime before it even happened. But it wasn't Eagle who had seen Ben that night – Mrs Taylor clicked the start button – it was those security
10 cameras.

Ben was the surprise star of the film. There he was in close-up, standing in front of the new gym building's wall. He was wearing the dark grey hoodie his mother had given him for his 14th birthday.
15 The image was in black and white but Ben saw it all in colour. He was shaking a can of red paint. He used red to write the outline of each letter. In a few minutes the words 'Catch Me' appeared on the wall. Everybody in the room was watching! Ben wished the film would stop.
20 He saw himself take another can out of the bag: it was the chrome colour. He used it to fill in the letters. You need a lot of paint to do that. That's why he had needed two cans. He remembered how proud he had been. It had looked so good!
25 It was all Jerry's fault. He was supposed to check the area for cameras. That was what Ben had asked him to do. The film was silent but Ben could hear the *clackclackclack* sound each time he shook one of the cans and the *pfsshhh* sound as he sprayed. He used the black paint to give each
30 letter a shadow – and yellow for highlights. Ben had practised for hours. How stupid it all seemed to him now. When he was finished, he stood back from the wall and

gave a thumbs up sign. He had even taken a selfie in front of his work with his phone.

Mrs Taylor clicked the pause button. She stopped the film at exactly the moment that Ben took off his mask. There he was staring stupidly at the security camera for all to see. Mr O'Reilly turned on the lights. Mrs Taylor cleared her throat and said in a very serious voice, "Ben, what we need to know now is: Who else was with you?"

"No one, Miss. I did it alone."

Mrs Taylor clicked the play button again and skipped a minute ahead. In this part of the film Ben was putting the cans back in his bag. "I'm sorry Ben," she said, "But I don't believe you." Mrs Taylor pointed at the screen. "See here," she said, "your lips are moving. It's perfectly clear to me that you are talking to someone."

"I often talk to myself," said Ben. One side of his mouth curled up into a smile.

"Ben!" said his mother sternly, "this is no time for jokes! Answer Mrs Taylor's question!"

"But I am telling the truth," insisted Ben. "There was no one else. If there were, he'd be on camera too." Eagle rolled his eyes.

"OK," Mrs Taylor sighed. "I can see we aren't going to get any further with this." She turned to Ben's parents. "Mr and Mrs Reckord, I'm sorry, but I have to tell you that Ben won't be allowed to come back to school for the rest of the school year. There's only one more week before the summer holidays. I must say, I'm really very disappointed. Ben has been doing well at school this year. I would never have expected something like this from him. This is all a complete surprise." Mrs Taylor paused. Everyone turned one last time to look at Ben's frozen image on the screen.

It seemed to Ben that the room itself sighed in disappointment.

Mrs Taylor continued, "When the summer holidays begin, Ben will have to come and clean off the graffiti and repaint the wall."

"Of course we'll cover all the costs," said Mrs Reckord in an apologetic way. Then Ben's parents thanked Mrs Taylor for giving him one more chance. They promised that Ben would have to 'answer for his actions'. They shook her hand, nodded to Mr O'Reilly, grabbed Ben by the arm and left the head teacher's office.

Later that night, after dinner, Ben's parents led him to the living room.

"Your mother and I have discussed the situation. We don't like punishing you, but this time …" began Ben's dad.

"We're both shocked at what you've done," his mum continued. "We think it's important that you take the time to think about it. That's why, for the next four days we don't want you to meet your friends or leave the house."

"What? I can't go out?! That's like being in prison!" shouted Ben.

"Don't raise your voice with me!" said his mother. Her eyes were bright and he could tell this was not the time to make any more trouble.

"You're lucky that Mrs Taylor is allowing you to return to school next year and that she didn't call the police! Do you even understand what you've done?"

Ben looked up at his mother, but said nothing.

"You destroy public property, you act like you don't care, you wear a dark hoodie and –"

"You gave it to me, Mum!"

"Don't interrupt me! You spray ugly graffiti across the school's new gym building! I just don't understand you! Your father and I are working so hard to give you everything you need! What more can we do?!"

Ben's mum looked like she was going to explode. "How could you have been so stupid to believe that you wouldn't get caught?!"

"That's just it, Mum, you're smart and I'm not!"

2 Welcome to the Shack

"So what's the plan?" Ying asked from the table in the centre of the room and looked across at The Mouth. He was standing next to the only window and looking through its dirty, broken glass.

The other members of the GROUP all waited for The Mouth's answer. Knuckles, only 15 years old, but 6 feet tall and with the body of a weightlifter, stood by the door. With his left hand, he felt the muscles in his right arm and looked round the room, an empty grin on his face. Jetta, next to Ying at the table, stared at her laptop, looked up quickly and then back down at the screen. Trixie sat down on an old box in the corner and took out her GROUP mobile.

"What are you looking at?" Ying asked. "I thought …"

"Oh, you've been thinking again, have you?" The Mouth interrupted. He walked over to the table and sat down next to Ying. A big smile lit up his dark face as he put his hand on her bare arm. Ying smiled back.

"Ying girl, haven't I told you a hundred times before to leave the thinking to the thinkers?"

Ying's smile disappeared in a flash. She looked down and her straight, black hair fell forward and hid her face. Then The Mouth got up again and went over to Knuckles.

"Knuckles," he said, "go out to the front gate and see if anyone is there."

"All right. And if there is someone there …?"

"Call me."

As Knuckles left the room, Trixie spoke for the first time.

"Who are you expecting?" she asked The Mouth. "We agreed we wouldn't tell anyone else about the Shack."

"I told you the other day … the girl at the skateboard park … remember?"

"Yeah, I remember," Trixie nodded. "So you told her where we meet? Just like that?"

"Don't worry!" The Mouth shook his head. "She's cool."

"What girl are you talking about?" Ying asked. "I don't remember any girl at the skateboard park."

"I don't tell you everything, Ying."

Jetta looked up from her laptop. "Bad idea, Mouth. She'll have a phone. The COMPANY can track that."

"I'm not stupid, Jetta. I told her she has to take the card out of her phone before she comes here … and anyway, you've checked her out online, haven't you?"

"Yeah," Jetta said. "I think she's OK."

"Well, I hope you're right," said Trixie and sat down on her box again and looked down at her phone.

The Mouth's phone rang and when Knuckles told him that there was a girl outside the Shack's front gate, he went to join his giant friend. They watched the girl through the

spy hole. She was wandering about and looking at the wall of the old, abandoned workshop that they called the Shack. She had a hoodie over her dyed black hair, a rucksack on her back and was carrying a skateboard. She
5 put the skateboard down and glided along the path and then returned and stopped in front of the gate. She came closer to the gate and looked carefully at it, as if she knew there was someone on the other side.

The Mouth nodded at Knuckles and he suddenly pulled
10 open the door, grabbed the girl by the arm and yanked her inside.

"Hey …" she started to shout but stopped when The Mouth held his finger to his lips.

"So you found us?" he said.

15 "Yes. It wasn't hard," the girl answered as she looked all over the workshop's yard.

"Welcome to the Shack. This is Knuckles. The others are inside. Come on," The Mouth said and waved the girl towards the door in the wall at the back of the yard.

20 "What's your name then?" Knuckles said as he followed the other two towards the door.

"Introductions inside, Knuckles," The Mouth told him. He opened the door and they all went inside.

As she entered the room, the skateboard girl looked
25 round at Ying, Jetta and Trixie who were all watching her. She could feel Ying's hostility and see it in her face too. Jetta almost smiled. Trixie looked worried. She spoke first.

"Have you taken the card out of your phone?" she asked.

30 "Yes," the girl answered and looked at The Mouth. "Like you told me." She pulled her phone and the SIM card out of a pocket in her rucksack to show them.

The Mouth smiled. "See? I told you she's cool. Meet Paige, everyone. Paige, you've already met Knuckles. This is Ying. This is …"

"Jetta," said Jetta before The Mouth could finish. "Hey."

5 "Hey," Paige said with a nod.

"I'm Trixie." The girl got up from her box and stood in front of Paige. "So how did you hear about us?"

Paige looked at The Mouth a little uncertainly. "Well, I just got talking to … I don't even know your name …"

10 "The Mouth," Knuckles said. "But his friends call him Moufie."

"Well, I just got talking to … The Mouth about stuff …"

"What stuff?" Trixie asked.

"Oh, you know, how people, like, can't live without 15 their mobile phones these days. They haven't got a real life any more. And the COMPANY's new personal assistant app, Perfect Pal, is making it even worse …"

"Do you have that app on your phone?" Trixie asked.

"No way!"

20 The Mouth interrupted them. "I told you Paige is cool, right? And we need more people in the GROUP. She thinks the same way about the COMPANY as we do."

"But you should have asked us first before you brought her here," Trixie said.

25 "Right," agreed Ying. "She could be a spy."

"A spy?" Paige looked at Ying in surprise. "What are you talking about? Who would I be a spy for?"

Ying stood up. "The COMPANY of course. What do you think?"

30 "For crying out loud, Ying, Jetta has checked her out," The Mouth shouted. "She's got nothing to do with the COMPANY! Right, Jetta?"

"Right," Jetta said. "But we should have talked about it first. Anyway, we can't do anything about that now. And we have work to do, remember? We're here to plan the hit at the shopping centre. So let's get started."

5   Paige listened as the members of the GROUP discussed their 'hit' at the shopping centre. The target was the COMPANY shop there. They had everything ready for that weekend but there was still one problem to solve.

"How do we hit the shop but not get caught?" The
10 Mouth asked. "That's what we still need to work out."

"There'll be customers inside," Jetta said.

"And security guards," Trixie added. "All their shops have security guards."

"There must be a way …" The Mouth went on.

15   But no one seemed to have the answer. They all looked at each other but no one said a word.

"A diversion." Paige's words broke the silence.

"What?" said Knuckles. "We aren't driving anywhere."

"No, Knuckles," Jetta said. "Paige is right. We need a
20 diversion to get people out of the shop …"

"… so that we can go in and hit it," The Mouth finished.

"But how can we create a diversion?" Trixie asked.

"Well," Paige began and suddenly all the GROUP's eyes were on her. "I have an idea. You see … I do a bit of magic
25 and …"

Paige explained her idea for a diversion while the others listened quietly. When she was finished The Mouth looked round in triumph. "See! I told you Paige was cool!"

3 The great escape

"*'Everything will be okay in the end. If it's not okay, then it's not the end.'* The singer, Ed Sheeran said that. Do you know his music, Ben?"

"Of course I do, and I don't like it – it's too … soft."

5   Jerry continued to read from his list. "*'The man who moves a mountain begins by carrying away small stones.'*"

"What is that supposed to mean? Who is stupid enough to want to move a mountain? It would hurt the environment."

10   "That was Confucius, Ben," replied Jerry.

"Yeah, you're right it was 'confusing'," said Ben and laughed at his own joke.

"Why are you laughing, Ben, I didn't want to confuse you. I can look up the meaning of that quote if you'd like."

15   "No, please don't."

"OK. Then I'll read you the next one. This is a very popular quote from Jim Rohn: *'Don't wish it were easier. Wish you were better.'* And here's your mum's favourite. *'Live life as though nobody is watching, and express yourself as*

20 *though everyone is listening.'* Nelson Mandela said that."

"Who told you to read these to me?"

"Nobody did, Ben, I found them online when I searched for 'quotes to make somebody feel better'."

"Well, they aren't working. All they're doing is giving

25 me a headache. I'd feel better if I could leave this room. Do you have any tips about how to do that? I'm sick of being a prisoner in my own home. And turn up the volume – I really like this song." It was an old reggae song his father often listened to: "*It takes a revolution, doo-a-doo-a, to make a*

solution, doo-a-doo-a. Too much confusion, so much frustration! Eh!"

Ben picked up the football next to his bed and bounced it several times against the white wall. Each time the ball hit the wall it made a small black mark. Ben noticed the marks and continued to bounce the ball against the wall in time with the music. *"I don't wanna live in the paaaark –* bam – *live in the park –* bam. *Can't trust no shadows after daaark –* bam – *shadows after dark –* bam, bam. *So my friend I wish that you could see –* bam – *like a bird in the tree –* bam, bam. *The prisoners must be free! Yeah!"*

When the song was over the wall was covered with little black marks. Ben kicked the ball under his bed.

"Jerry, is Aniela still here?"

"Just a moment, Ben. I'll check the house schedule for you … Yes, Ben, she is here until 4 pm. Shall I call her for you?"

"No, I just wanted to know if she's still in the house." Ben walked towards the door.

"What are you going to do, Ben?"

"Nothing. I'll be back soon." Ben left his room. He heard voices and followed them to the kitchen. But it was just the TV. Aniela had probably forgotten to turn it off. He ran up the stairs to the second floor. The steps were covered with thick, soft carpet so his steps made no sound. He tiptoed down the wide hall, past the home gym and the video room to his parent's bedroom. He heard Aniela singing a song as she worked. He carefully opened the door and peeked in. Aniela was just putting clean sheets on the king size bed. The vacuum cleaner was lying on the floor like a sleeping dog. Ben saw his reflection in the mirror that covered the opposite wall. *She'll be working in this room for a while – now's my chance!*

Ben ran back to his room and grabbed a jacket and his phone, which lit up when he picked it up.

"Where are we going, Ben?" asked Jerry.

"We're going to make our great escape, my friend."

"I don't think this is a good idea, Ben. You might get into trouble."

"How can my parents punish me any more than they already have? I have to get out of here. Don't worry, Jerry, we'll be back before Aniela leaves."

Ben ran into the kitchen. The window above the kitchen sink was open, as always. Ben climbed onto the counter, stepped in the sink, crawled through the open window and jumped down to the street below.

4 Watching people

Melanie Reckord took the lift up to the 39th floor and walked quickly to her large office. She had a lot of work to finish and there simply weren't enough hours in a day to do it all. She sat down at her desk and tapped the 'Home view' button on her tablet screen. A list of all the rooms in the house appeared. She selected 'Ben's room'. A live view of Ben's room appeared on the screen. She saw the pile of clothes on the floor and some strange marks on his wall.

"A royal mess as usual," she said. One by one, she then checked every room in the house: the kitchen, the dining room, the gym, the home cinema, her own bedroom with

Aniela, who was now vacuuming the floor, and finally street view. *Where is that boy?* she wondered.

She sat back and thought about what to do next. She tapped a button labelled 'Jerry', then 'send message' and typed: "Send full activity report. Home by 5". She put on her headset, tapped on the phone symbol, then 'contacts' and 'Steve Reckord'.

"Hi Melanie, what's up?"

"It's Ben – I think he's sneaked out of the house. I'd go home and check, but I have to finish these reports for Perfect Pal Plus by this evening."

"Don't worry, he's only 14 after all. I certainly wasn't an angel at his age either," said Mr Reckord in a comforting voice. "He's probably in the garden."

"Maybe. I just hope he's not up to any mischief. Anyway, I've asked Jerry to send us a full report. But, still, we'll have to have a hard talk with Ben this evening. He's really going through a bad phase. I just wish that he could have picked a better time to act up. We both have so much to do before the launch."

"Listen, darling, let me talk to him tonight – alone. You can stay in the office as long as you like."

"OK, maybe that's a good idea. He usually listens to you. I'll be home at about 8 then. I can't sleep here, you know!"

"Of course not. Don't work too hard and please, *don't worry*. Jerry and I have it all under control."

Mrs Reckord tapped the 'end call' button, took off her head set and turned to her computer. She scrolled to the end of the document on the screen and started typing.

As Ben walked down the street he looked back at the open kitchen window and noticed the small security camera on the side of the building.

"Jerry, what was my mother's favourite quote again: *'Live life as though nobody is watching …'*"

"Yes, good, Ben. *'Live life as though nobody is watching and express yourself as though everyone is listening.'* And I think you'll like this one too: *'Learn the rules like a pro, so you can break them like an artist.'* Pablo Picasso said that."

"Not bad."

"Shall I read the next one, Ben?"

"No, that's enough. I've got one of my own: Choose freedom at any cost!"

"I've recorded that for you Ben."

"Good, thanks. I might need it later."

"Where do you want to go Ben?"

"If I have to spend the next three days cooped up in my room, I need some new video games. Can you suggest a good place to buy them?"

"OK, I'm checking that for you. The electronics shop at Eden Square has a big sale today, Ben."

"Good. Let's go."

"You need to take the number 59 bus at …"

"I know how to get there. Just put on some music."

"What do you want to hear, Ben."

"Something loud, hard, with a good fast beat."

Ben got off the bus. It was lunchtime and the square was full of people. He walked toward the centre of the square and sat down on the edge of the fountain.

"The electronics shop is on the other side of Eden Square, Ben," said Jerry.

"I can see it."

"Why aren't you going there then, Ben?"

"I'm watching people. Like that homeless man there. He's going up to all those people and asking for money. He's even trying to get them to buy an old magazine. But no one is paying attention to him."

"Why not, Ben?"

"Why are you asking me? I don't know. I suppose he probably hasn't washed in weeks. He must stink." Ben scanned the names of the shops on the square. There was a Jeans shop, a fish and chip shop and one of the COMPANY's shops.

Ben's parents worked for the COMPANY. His mum was a lawyer and his father developed software and security systems.

An interesting looking girl stopped in front of the COMPANY shop. She had a large rucksack on her back and was carrying a small folding table.

"What time is it, Jerry?"

"It's already 12:30, Ben – we should go and buy those video games and then go back home. Aniela has probably noticed that you're not at home, Ben. She might call your parents."

But Ben wasn't listening. He was watching that girl. She had dyed black hair and very pale skin. She wore a black hoodie over a short black skirt and black army boots.

"Ben – I've looked up the price of 10 different video games. There's a NetWorlds 2 game for only £18 and …"

Ben turned down the volume of his phone and walked up to the girl's table. He was curious to see what she would do next.

5 The magic hit

"Don't worry, you'll do just great," The Mouth said and gave Paige a big smile.

"Hurry up, Moufie," hissed Ying. "We have to go."

The Mouth ignored Ying, gave Paige a thumbs up and
5 said, "See you later at the Shack."

Paige watched The Mouth, Trixie and Ying walk towards the shopping centre. As they reached the corner, Ying turned round and looked back angrily at Paige. Paige just shook her head, picked up her table and walked slowly
10 after them. She wondered where Knuckles was. When she turned the corner into Eden Square, the others were already gone.

Paige walked along to the big COMPANY shop and set up her table in front of the shop window with all its
15 adverts. ONE PHONE FOR THE WHOLE WORLD. NO MORE LONELY DAYS OR NIGHTS – WITH PERFECT PAL, YOU'LL ALWAYS HAVE COMPANY.

She put her sign on the table: Matches' Magic Show. Then she put her hat for money in front of it and got
20 everything else that she needed out of her bag: the cards, the coins, the small cups and larger boxes.

When she started on her magic routine, a few people stopped to watch: an old man with a walking stick, a young boy with his mother.

25 "Look, mummy, she's doing magic like on TV!"

Soon five or six people, a small crowd, stood in front of her table. At the end of every trick the little boy clapped, the old man smiled kindly and a teenage boy in a bright blue jacket, with a COMPANY phone in his hand, shook his head and rolled his eyes.

OK, Paige thought and gave him a hard look. *I know I'm not very good yet, you tosser, so why don't you just …*

5 Suddenly Paige felt that someone was standing behind her. She turned round quickly to see Knuckles. He was dressed as usual in an army pullover and trousers. He moved his face towards her and gave her a horrible smile.

She saw the big gap in his front teeth and felt his hot
10 breath on her face.

Knuckles pulled a five pound note out of his trouser pocket and held it up.

"See this?" he said.

"Yes," Paige nodded at him. "It's a five-pound note."

15 "Right," Knuckles agreed. "I bet you a fiver I can work out how you do your next trick. If I'm right, I win a fiver from you. If you win, you get this." He waved the money around for everyone to see.

Paige looked at the coins in her hat and said, "All right."

She took a pack of cards and spread them across her table so that everyone could see they were normal playing cards. She picked them up and began to shuffle them. Then she held them out to Knuckles. "Pick a card," she said to him, "any card."

Knuckles picked a card from the pack.

"Now, don't let me see the card, but show it to everyone else, so they can see what it is."

As Paige went on with her trick she thought, *This is the easiest trick in the world, but I don't think Knuckles will get it …*

At the end of the trick, Paige put one card after another on the table. "Not that one," she said. "Not that one. Not that one …"

Finally she looked up at Knuckles as she put the Queen of Spades on the table for everyone to see. "Was that your card?" she asked. "The Queen of Spades?"

Everyone in the crowd began to clap and Paige smiled at the big boy in his army clothes. Knuckles didn't smile back.

"No," he said. "That wasn't my card."

The crowd booed him. "Don't be a cheat," the old man said. "Give the young lady her fiver."

"Don't you call me a cheat," Knuckles threatened. "She's the only cheat here."

"Cheat, cheat, cheat," the crowd began to chant and Knuckles went wild. He put his hands under Paige's table and threw it into the air. Her cards, her hat, coins and boxes flew everywhere. Suddenly everyone was shouting. The noise was so loud that all the customers, the shop assistants and a security guard came out of the COMPANY shop to find out what was happening.

"Oi!" the guard shouted at Knuckles as he stood over Paige who was picking her things up off the ground. "Get lost, will you! You're scaring our customers away."

"You get lost!" Knuckles shouted. He walked over, 5 grabbed the guard's hat and ran off along the street. The security guard started to run after him but soon stopped. He turned back to Paige.

"Hurry up," he told her. "Pack up and get out of here. And don't let me catch you here again, or I'll call the 10 police."

Then he spoke to the big crowd of customers outside the shop.

"Sorry about that, ladies and gents, but the show's over now, so if you'd like to go back inside ..."

15 Slowly, the crowd of COMPANY customers started to move into the shop again. The security guard followed

them, and as he entered the shop his hand flew up to his mouth.

"What the ...? Who did that?"

Paige had all her things together again now and went to look in the shop too. Across the walls, and the counters, she could see slogans in big, bright red letters: "EVERY TEXT YOU SEND, EVERY CALL YOU MAKE, WE'LL BE WATCHING YOU! THE COMPANY" the slogans said. "YOUR PERFECT PAL IS THE COMPANY'S PERFECT SPY!" And "DUMP YOUR COMPANY PHONE! DO IT TODAY! THE GROUP"

Next to every slogan was the GROUP's tag: "THEY'RE WATCHING YOU"

A big smile spread across Paige's face. "Yes!" she said under her breath, clenched her fist and started to walk away. She stopped when the teenager in the bright blue jacket stood in her way. He held out a five pound note to her. She took it automatically.

"Here," the boy said, "you won this. That kid had no idea how you did that trick."

Then he turned round and walked quickly away before Paige could say a word. She just stood there and watched him with her mouth open. When he disappeared round a corner she looked down at the note in her hands. Next to the picture of the Queen was a telephone number, the name Ben, and a smiley face.

"Ben!"

"I'm in the kitchen, Dad!" Ben shouted. He took seven hot mini-pizzas out of the oven as his dad's smiling face appeared at the kitchen door.

5   "Someone's hungry! Didn't Aniela make you lunch today?"

"I'm 14, Dad, I can make my own lunch. I just wasn't hungry earlier." Ben put all seven pizzas on a large plate, and sat down at the kitchen counter.

10   "Well, can I join you? I skipped lunch too and I'm starving. Your mother won't be home until later."

Ben pushed one mini-pizza in his dad's direction before nearly swallowing half a pizza in one bite. With a mouthful of pizza he tried to warn his father: "Car-fu--, Da-, iss rea-y
15 –ot!"

Mr Reckord held his fingers over the pizza.

"You can say that again." Mr Reckord smiled. "So, what did you do today?"

"Not much … what do you expect? I've been cooped up
20 at home all day so I wasn't exactly able to have great adventures."

"Right, of course, I understand."

"Really? Do you? What did you do today, Dad?" asked Ben in a sarcastic tone.

25   "Oh … me … well … as you know your mother and I are working very hard to be ready for the launch of the COMPANY's newest product – Perfect Pal Plus. So, today my department was running the final tests to see if the

system works as it should. We really don't want anything to go wrong at next week's launch."

Mr Reckord finally took a bite of the pizza and pretended to remember something. "Hey! That reminds me – we were lucky enough to get a ticket for you to attend the launch too!"

Ben clapped his hands like a little child. "I'm so excited!" he said in the same sarcastic tone.

Mr Reckord shook his head and took another bite of pizza. "Well, you're coming, so that's that. It's a very important event and it means a lot to both of us. We've both put a lot of work into this project."

He got up and filled two glasses with a soft drink from the fridge. They heard the house door open and slam shut.

"There's your mother now." Mr Reckord pushed the half eaten pizza back onto Ben's plate. "Take this, please," he whispered. "She won't be too pleased that I've started without her."

Mrs Reckord entered the kitchen and with a heavy sigh dropped her briefcase and laptop on the kitchen counter.

"Have you darlings left anything for me? I really can't face cooking after a day like today."

"Ben was kind enough to give me one of his little snacks. But I haven't really eaten. Why don't we order an Indian takeaway – or sushi? That way you, I mean, we won't have to cook or clean. What about you, Ben? Can you squeeze in a little Chicken Tikka Masala after all those pizzas?"

"No, thank you. I'm going back to my room."

"OK. Goodnight, Ben, and sleep well," said Mr Reckord with a large smile.

"So did you speak to him?" whispered Mrs Reckord as soon as Ben was out of earshot.

"Well, I did tell him about next week's launch – and I was very firm that he must come with us."

5 "And what about today? Did you find out where he was?"

"Not exactly. I mean I did ask him, but …"

"Well, it's very clear to me why we need Perfect Pal Plus."

10 "What do you mean?"

"Most parents today are too scared to find out the truth! And you are a great example of a scared-as-a-rabbit parent! Why do you just accept his lies?!" Mrs Reckord angrily opened the cupboard, took out a glass and put it down on 15 the counter with a bang. She then grabbed the bottle of soft drink and poured some into the glass. It quickly ran over the top and made a little pink puddle on the kitchen counter.

"Oh damn!" she exclaimed.

20 "Calm down, Melanie! You shouldn't get so upset! The important thing is that Ben is at home now, he's safe and you and I can relax a bit."

"All I can say, Steve, is that I'm really glad we have Jerry. I wouldn't know what to do without those activity 25 reports. It calms me down you know. I suppose every mother worries about her child. I'm just trying to do the right thing …"

"Of course you are. We both are. I want Ben to trust me. That's why I didn't push too hard. He has to have 30 some secrets of his own. We all have to."

"Well I won't make any secret of the fact that I really don't trust him right now. He doesn't want us to know what he's doing." Mrs Reckord took a sip of the pink drink. "Oh God," she moaned.

"What's wrong?"

"I'm starving! I could eat for three! Let's call that
5 takeaway place … NOW!" Mrs Record reached into her handbag for her phone. "Find the nearest Indian takeaway, please." She kissed her husband's cheek and grabbed a cloth to clean up the spilled drink.

7 Wake-up call

As The Mouth, Ying and Trixie approached the Shack's
10 front gate, Trixie got out her GROUP phone and punched in some numbers. With a quiet click, the gate opened. Inside, Jetta was waiting for them.

"There's already news about the hit online," she said.

"And photos?" The Mouth asked.

15 "And photos – look." Jetta turned her laptop round so that the others could see the screen. It showed the back of a security guard as he looked into the COMPANY shop with the GROUP's big red letters across the wall: EVERY TEXT YOU SEND, EVERY CALL YOU MAKE, WE'LL BE
20 WATCHING YOU! THE COMPANY. The Mouth clicked through more photos, then pumped his fist in the air. "Yes! And there's our GROUP tag too. They won't like that."

Ying came over to The Mouth and the two clapped their hands together in a high-five. "We showed them," she
25 said. "Wow, that was so exciting. We have to celebrate!"

"Yeah, that was a really good hit. Well done, guys," Jetta said and turned her laptop back. "But don't get too excited. This won't be on the telly or any of the big online news sites, so not many people are going to see these photos. And we can't spread them on social media ourselves. That would lead THE COMPANY straight to us."

5 Suddenly, the door opened with a bang and Knuckles came in. He had a big smile on his face and a plastic bag full of coke bottles. He danced round the room and handed everyone a bottle.

"Were we good or were we good? Cheers!" he shouted, 10 held his bottle to his lips and drank it half empty in a couple of seconds.

The Mouth banged his bottle against the one in Knuckles' giant fist. "You were brilliant, mate."

"We were all brilliant," Ying said.

15 "Right. But we're not all here yet," The Mouth went on.

"Oh, yes," said Jetta. "Where's Paige, the magic lady?"

"Does she know the code for the gate?" Trixie asked.

"She hasn't even got a GROUP phone yet, so she can't 20 get in," Jetta answered. "She's probably outside right now."

Knuckles put his bottle down on the table and went out into the yard to look through the spy hole. A little while later he came back in. Paige was right behind him.

The Mouth went straight over to her, took her by the 25 hand and led her into the centre of the room. "Congratulations, Paige, you were a real star. Big hand for Paige, everyone. No, a big hand for all of us!" The whole GROUP clapped and cheered.

When the clapping stopped, Trixie said, "We did really 30 well today – and this is only the beginning. Like Jetta says, maybe not many people will notice today's hit. But I've got an idea for our next one." She held up her phone. On it the others could see an advert for the launch of the COMPANY's latest product – a version of Perfect Pal especially for young people, Perfect Pal Plus.

"Let's hit THE COMPANY on their own home ground," Trixie went on. "Then people will really start to notice us – and listen to us."

Again, everyone cheered – everyone except Jetta.

"I don't want to spoil the party," she said, "but I think we have more important things to do than spray paint in COMPANY shops and stuff like that. That sort of thing won't really hurt the COMPANY and one day, you know, they might catch us. Or get photos of us and find out who we are. Look at this."

Jetta turned her laptop around again so that the others could see. It was another photo of the COMPANY shop with their red lettering all over. A security guard was moving some customers toward the door. Next to the door, outside, they could see the back of someone's head. It was a girl with black hair. She was looking into the shop. Paige gasped as she recognized herself.

"What about it?" The Mouth asked.

"Can't you see?" Jetta said. "The girl outside the shop. Don't you recognize her?"

"It could be anyone," Trixie said. "You can only see the back of her head."

"Maybe," Jetta said, "but the COMPANY security people will look at all the footage from all the security cameras all round that area and then maybe they'll find a better picture of that girl with black hair. What then?"

"But we were careful that there were no cameras on us when I was doing the magic show," Paige said.

"Right," said The Mouth.

"Yes, but what about when you were walking there and walking back?" Jetta asked and looked round at all the others. "Can you be sure there were no cameras on you anywhere?"

5   No one said a word.

After a few moments, Trixie asked Jetta, "OK, then, what's more important than messing up the COMPANY's events and getting in the news?"

"We need to find out a lot more about what the
10 COMPANY is doing with Perfect Pal. How they're spying on everyone, how they're recording everything we do or say. How Perfect Pal is sending all our information back to the COMPANY so that they can control us all."

"And when we know all that," The Mouth asked, "what
15 do we do then?"

Jetta stood up. "We tell people. We put it out on the internet so that they can't hide it. We have to wake the public up."

"Right," Trixie nodded her head in agreement. "We
20 have to wake the public up. But we can't do that with just a lot of information that goes in one ear and out the other. We have to do something that will really hit the headlines. That will be a wake-up call for the public. I say we hit the Perfect Pal Plus launch."

25   "Yeah," Ying shouted. "Let's do it."

The Mouth gave a thumbs up and said, "Watch out, COMPANY, here we come!"

Then everyone cheered and clapped again – everyone except Jetta. She shook her head, picked up her laptop
30 and walked out.

8 The tower hit

Ben got into the back of the long dark Mercedes and slumped into the comfortable seat. His parents were talking non-stop in the front as they drove through the city to the centre of town.

5 "I'm so excited about tonight's launch, Steve."

"Well, you've been working hard on this project for months, Melanie, ..."

"So have you. Where would Perfect Pal Plus be without you software engineers?"

10 "Yeah, we've both worked hard on this, so let's have fun tonight. We deserve it."

Ben put his earphones in so that he could no longer hear them. He chose shuffle on his music app and told Jerry to turn up the volume. Jerry tried to suggest a music 15 genre but Ben just ignored him.

45 minutes later they were on the top floor of the COMPANY tower. Ben looked out at all the lights of the city below – and then at all the boring COMPANY employees, PR people, radio and TV reporters all around 20 him. At least the food was good. He walked over to one of the young waiters who stood there with a tray full of delicacies. He picked up a mini-sandwich, looked at the waiter for a second and walked away towards the bar for a drink. *That waiter – I've seen him before somewhere ...*

25 He got a drink and went over to the window. He looked down at the city and saw a COMPANY advert on another tall building. Suddenly he remembered where he had seen the waiter before: at Eden Square, when that girl was doing her magic tricks. *Matches and her magic tricks.* He was

the kid who tried to cheat the girl and then went crazy and knocked her table over.

It took a little while before he found the waiter again just as he disappeared through a door at the end of a corridor. Ben hurried towards the door but before he could open it a security guard stopped him. "I'm sorry. You can't go in there, I'm afraid. It's just the kitchen. The toilets are the other way."

In the COMPANY's top-floor kitchen, Ying was washing dishes at a sink. Knuckles tapped her on the shoulder and whispered in her ear. Then they both looked round to see if anybody was watching and walked over to the service lift. The lift door opened quietly and they slipped inside. Knuckles took off his apron and threw it over the camera in the top corner of the lift. Soon they were on their way down to the underground car park.

When the lift doors opened again they walked past the expensive German cars and up the ramp to the exit. They opened the small door to the side of the car exit and let The Mouth and Jetta in.

Jetta carried her laptop and a bag full of equipment.

"OK, Ying," The Mouth said, "you wait here at the door. Trixie and Paige are outside with the bikes. If there's a problem, text me a 'T' for trouble."

Ying nodded and The Mouth, Knuckles and Jetta ran quickly to the lift, went inside and the door closed.

In a small office many floors below the launch event, Jetta plugged her laptop into the COMPANY system. While she worked, The Mouth and Knuckles stood guard at the door.

"You'd better go back upstairs," The Mouth told Knuckles. "People will wonder where you are. We'll meet you outside at the bikes."

Knuckles walked along the corridor to the service lift and pulled away the chair that they had put in the doorway to keep the lift there. 30 seconds later, as the door opened on the 60th floor, he pulled his apron off the camera, quickly put it on again, and walked out into the kitchen. Without a word to anyone, he took a tray of drinks and went out to serve the guests again.

On the stage at the end of the big hall, the COMPANY's top manager, Richard Sykes, stood in front of a big screen. He put on a microphone headset and tapped it to get the crowd's attention.

"Can you all hear me?" he asked.

The crowd all clapped and cheered. When the noise died down, Sykes went on: "To be honest, I don't know how I managed before I got my Perfect Pal personal assistant. I call her Alice after my gran."

"Mine is called Alice too," shouted someone from the crowd.

"My gran Alice," Sykes continued, "used to manage my life for me when I was a small boy. I relied on her. So did my parents. And you know, young people do need a bit of management sometimes. Well, my kids do anyway – but their grandmothers both live thousands of miles away across the sea, so they can't help us. That's why Perfect Pal is getting an upgrade for kids. Let me introduce you to Perfect Pal Plus."

As the crowd began to clap again, he clicked the small remote in his left hand and a slide came up on the big screen behind him. It showed a teenage girl who was holding a brand new COMPANY phone as she walked off into a big city night. Above the picture a large caption read: YOUR CHILD WILL NEVER BE ALONE AGAIN. STAY SAFE WITH PERFECT PAL PLUS.

5 In the crowd, Ben rolled his eyes. *Kids need freedom, not 'management'.* He soon stopped listening to the manager's presentation and looked around the room. His eyes stopped wandering when he saw Knuckles again, off to the side with a tray of drinks. *There you are,* he thought.
10 *You won't get away this time.* Slowly, Ben started to move through the crowd towards Knuckles who was staring at the stage.

Ben was concentrating so hard on Knuckles that it took a little time before he noticed that the crowd was starting
15 to shout and boo. People were pointing at the screen and there were flashes everywhere as they took photos with their cameras and phones. Knuckles had a big grin on his face now, his eyes still on the screen. Ben took a photo of Knuckles with his own phone and pressed 'Upload'. Then
20 he turned his own eyes to the stage and screen again.

Richard Sykes had turned his back to the crowd and was clicking his remote frantically. There were some security people with him. But they couldn't change the slide. It was another photo of a girl with a phone in her
25 hand. But this girl was almost naked, just in bra and panties. The caption above her was different too. In big red letters it said: YOUR CHILD WILL HAVE NO SECRETS WITH PERFECT PAL PLUS. THE COMPANY'S PERFECT SPY WILL LISTEN TO EVERY CALL SHE MAKES, READ
30 EVERY TEXT SHE SENDS. DUMP PERFECT PAL PLUS TODAY. THE GROUP.

THEY'RE WATCHING YOU.

Ben felt a grin on his own lips. He looked back to Knuckles again. *He was there when the GROUP sprayed graffiti in that shop and he's here again now – that can't be a coincidence.*

Knuckles was moving now, walking away along a corridor. Ben pushed through the crowd and followed him. Knuckles went through a door to the stairs. Everybody else in the crowd was still watching the screen, so nobody saw Ben as he followed. As he opened the door, he heard a crash. Knuckles had thrown his tray on the floor and was already running down the stairs. But Ben was faster. He ran after Knuckles and caught him two floors down. Knuckles turned suddenly and his strong arms pushed Ben against the wall.

"What do you want?" Knuckles said and pushed his face very close to Ben's.

"I remember you," Ben said. "You cheated that girl who was doing magic tricks at Eden Square."

"So? What's it to you?"

Ben looked Knuckles in the eye. "I gave her the five pounds she won – so you owe me five pounds now."

Knuckles' mouth opened in a wide grin that showed the gap in his teeth. "Don't be a nerd, mate. Pai… er … she didn't want the five pounds."

"What do you mean? How do you know that? What? Oh, I see, you know her. Matches was her name, right?"

"Look, I've wasted enough time with you already. I'm going to let you go now and you're going to walk back upstairs and forget all about me. If not, I'll put your head through the wall the next time I see you, OK?"

"You're in the GROUP, aren't you? I've got your photo, you know," Ben said.

"What?" Knuckles looked worried. "Gimme your phone!"

"That won't help. I've already uploaded the photo to my computer at home. Is Matches in the GROUP too?"

5 Ben could see the concern in Knuckles' wide face. "If you don't give me that girl's number," Ben continued, "I'll send your photo to the COMPANY's security people."

Knuckles let go of Ben and stood there for a while before he took Ben's phone out of the boy's pocket and 10 held it in his hand for a few seconds. Then he raised his hand as if he was going to smash the phone on the floor. Instead, he just swiped the screen and tapped in a number, gave the phone back to Ben and ran down the stairs.

9 The call

For the hundredth time, Ben tapped Matches' name on his 15 contact list. The screen displayed three options: call / send text message / view contact.

"Just do it!" said Jerry.

"Who asked you for your opinion?"

"Nobody asked me, Ben. I'm just tired of you tapping 20 me in the same place over and over again – I'm getting chest pains!" Jerry chuckled in a mechanical way, which irritated Ben even more.

Paige carefully brushed the black nail polish on her left thumbnail. She held up her hand and blew on her nails to 25 make it dry faster. There was no GROUP meeting today and she really didn't want to practise her magic tricks again. Paige emptied her rucksack and shook out the chewing gum wrappers and bread crumbs over the rubbish bin. She opened her purse. She only had that 5-pound note that boy had given her. She took it out, carefully unfolded it and read what he had written.

Ben – his name is Ben. Then she checked the hair dye instructions again. *OK. Five more minutes and I have to wash this stuff off.* Her mobile rang.

"Hello?"

"Matches?" said a hesitant voice.

"Who?"

"Is this Matches? Hi … uh … This is Ben. Remember? Eden Square – two weeks ago."

"Ben? That's soooo strange! I was just looking at your number. But, wait a second, how did you get mine? I didn't give it to you."

"It just appeared in my phone … like magic!"

"Magic? I don't know if I like that kind of magic. It's suspicious. So come on, tell me. I want to know."

"Well, suppose I'm a good detective. I checked all the city listings for magicians … and I found your name and number."

"Good try. Now try telling me the truth."

"All right. Someone you know gave it to me."

"And you don't want to tell me who it is, right?"

"All I can say is that he's tall and he's mean and I risked my life to get it." Paige couldn't believe her ears – was this for real or just a prank call.

"How old are you?" she asked.

"Fourteen."

"Full name?"

"Ben William Reckord."

"Address?"

Paige typed the information into a search engine. She found the name of his school and looked at his house with 'street view'. *Nice neighbourhood ...*, she thought.

"OK. Last question: why are you calling me?"

"I was wondering if you'd like to ... maybe, I mean, what are you doing? I mean, would you like to meet or ...?"

"Meet you? When?"

"Like now."

Now? He wants to meet right now ... The hair dye was starting to make her head tingle and she felt a bit drip down her neck.

"How about in an hour?" she said. "But where?"

"What about Eden Square? By the fountain."

"Yeah, OK. 3 pm, Eden Square fountain..." Ben heard a click.

"Bye ..." he said softly to the dial tone.

Paige smiled. *He thinks my name is Matches! That's funny. What a weirdo! Uh-oh ... Time's up! I have to rinse this stuff out of my hair now!*

Paige rushed to the shower.

10 Trust

Ben arrived at Eden Square a few minutes before three. He leaned against a lamp post and waited. He had a good view of the fountain and the square's large clock from there.

15:09.

Is she even going to show up? he wondered.

Then he heard a strange scraping sound behind him and quickly turned around. Matches came to a slow stop and hopped off her skateboard.

5 "You're a skateboarder?" Ben asked as if surprised.

"No, where did you get that idea?" She laughed, set her board down on the ground and rolled it back and forth with one foot. "Yeah, I started skating a few months ago … I don't have to use the underground anymore. So I save
10 lots of money. And anyway, I don't live very far away from here, so it's easy."

As she spoke, Ben studied every part of her pretty face. She had bright green eyes, and a small, serious mouth which suddenly broke into a broad smile. He also noticed
15 the two silver skulls that dangled from her ears, and the ring in her bottom lip which moved up and down as she talked.

"What about you?" asked Paige.

"Me? Skateboarding? Yeah, I used to – about two years
20 ago. That's all I did back then."

Paige had no trouble imagining Ben on a skateboard. He was tall and slim and was wearing a faded orange T-shirt over loose grey trousers. She liked his face and the warm brown colour of his skin.

25 "You must be really good then. I can't even do a good Ollie, yet."

Ben shrugged his shoulders.

"Hey," Paige said and handed him her board, "why don't you show me some tricks?"

30 Ben hesitated. "OK, but it's been a really long time. I'll probably fall on my face!" He stepped on the board and rode towards the fountain. He picked up speed and moved

his right foot to the back of the board and shifted his left foot just behind the front wheels; the skateboard rose off the ground and then back down again.

"Not bad!" shouted Paige. Ben smiled, performed the
5 move again and then rode right into a group of pigeons. They stopped their search for bread crumbs and flew up into the sky. Ben continued around the fountain and nearly rode into a woman who was walking across the square with her two young children.

10 "Hey, watch out!" she shouted angrily. Ben apologized and quickly rode back to Paige.

"I'd better stop before there's a serious accident," he said and handed the board back to Paige.

"No, no, you're really good! Show me more!"

15 Ben shook his head. "Maybe later – there are too many people here. But I know some really cool spots where we can go later. Anyway, are you hungry? I mean, we could have a pizza or something."

"Yeah, OK. But it has to be cheap."

20 "Don't worry about that, I can pay. So, what do you like? Chinese? Indian? Pizza?"

"I don't know. How about that fish and chip shop over there?" Fish and chips was the one fast food Ben really didn't like.

25 "Sounds good," Ben said. His phone vibrated in his pocket. It was a message from Jerry:

But Ben, you hate fish and chips! I've searched
for other options in the area and found these:
1 Pizza Roma ★★★★☆ (66 reviews)
30 2 Route 66 Burgers ★★★☆☆ (43 reviews)
I would recommend the pizza place because –

Ben didn't read the rest and followed Paige into the 'Fish club'. They found an empty table and sat down. Paige ordered fish and chips while Ben asked for a large portion of chips and a coke.

5   They first spoke about school.

"It's so boring!" said Paige shaking her head. "The kids at school are always talking to their phones during the breaks – they really don't see what's going on around them."

10   Ben proudly told her about the graffiti episode and how he was suspended from school. "My parents were really angry – my mum nearly hit the roof!"

"Yeah, my mum was not pleased when I came home with this …" Paige pointed to her bottom lip piercing. "But
15 she got used to it – now she doesn't mind the way I dress."

"That's cool," said Ben, "My mum hasn't calmed down yet. I wasn't even allowed out but I sneaked out anyway. That's when I saw your show. By the way … why weren't you in school that day?"

20   "I don't always go to school," said Paige mysteriously.

Ben wasn't sure if she was telling the truth. "And what did your parents say?" he asked.

"You mean my mum? She didn't find out about it." Paige looked down at her plate and broke a chip into two
25 pieces.

Ben tried to change the subject. "Hey," he began, "did you see what the GROUP sprayed in the company store?"

"Yeah, of course and I'm all for it."

"Really? I'm not so sure … I mean everybody has a
30 Perfect Pal – so what's the problem? It's not really about Big Brother control, you know."

"Yes it is. The COMPANY is trying to control and influence everything we do."

"Oh come on, it's not like that … Here, let me show you." Ben took out his phone and laid it on the table. "OK. Name one of your favourite songs."

"Why? What for?"

"Just do it," said Ben with a sly smile.

"OK, 'In transit' by Girl Bang."

"Jerry, please play 'In transit' by Girl Bang."

"OK, Ben, I'm searching for it. Just a moment." Seconds later the song started playing. Everyone in the restaurant turned around and stared at them. The restaurant manager came over to their table,

"Do you kids realise that there are other people in here? Turn that off, or I'll have to ask you to leave! All right?" He gave them an angry look and walked away.

Ben rolled his eyes, but he tapped on his phone and the music stopped.

Paige shook her head. "Thanks for the demonstration, but I know what a personal assistant can do – I wasn't born yesterday, you know."

"Yes, but …"

Paige ignored Ben and continued. "I certainly don't want 'a friend' who wants me to buy as much as I can, and who sends activity reports about every stupid little thing that I do to my parents and …"

Ben held up his hand. "Hey calm down … don't get so upset. You almost sound like you're a member of the GROUP. Are you?"

"And what if I am?" Paige pushed back the hair that had fallen across her face. "I'm not ready to give away my privacy … and certainly not to the COMPANY! Don't you know that they're always listening in! They probably even know that you're sitting here with me."

"But you still haven't answered my question – are you part of the GROUP?"

"Yes!" Paige blurted out. "We need to wake people up to what's really going on!"

Just at that moment, Jerry lit up and added: "Right on, Paige! 'Choose freedom at any cost!' Those are Ben's exact words which I recorded ten days ago at 11:21 am."

Ben tapped on the 'shut down Perfect Pal' button.

Jerry managed to squeeze in a last word: "Don't do that, Ben. I can help ..."

Paige's face hardened. She looked away.

"Sorry, Paige. It's really off now."

Paige didn't answer. She was angry with herself. She had said much too much.

"I saw what you guys did at the Perfect Pal Plus launch. I was there."

"You were there? Why?"

"My parents work for the COMPANY. My dad is a software developer and my mum is a lawyer. I try out all their new products – at least the ones for kids." Ben looked down at his plate.

Why did I tell her that? Now she's never going to want to see me again. Ben shoved his hands deep into his pockets. His fingers pushed against his phone. Suddenly Jerry's voice spoke up from below the table.

"Should I play another song, Ben?"

Paige stood up to leave.

"But ... no! Wait! It was just an accident. I didn't mean to turn it on again. Please! Wait!" Ben pulled his phone out of his pocket and set it on the table. "Please! I want to hear more about the GROUP. I really want to listen!"

"I'm sure you do – you're probably recording every word I say."

5 "No!" protested Ben. "That's not true!" But it was too late. Paige had already left the shop. Ben tried to run after her, but the manager stopped him.

"Hey! You pay first and run after your girlfriend later!"

All the way home, Ben was really angry: with Jerry, with 10 his parents, with himself and even with Paige.

She shouldn't have just run away.

"Why does everything get so complicated?" he said out loud.

"Would you like to hear some relaxing music, Ben?" 15 asked Jerry.

"Who asked you?" shouted Ben. "I wasn't talking to you. In fact, I don't know why I've ever said anything to you – you're just an annoying piece of software!"

Ben passed a rubbish bin and tossed in his phone. It 20 landed on top of some smelly and wet newspapers.

"Stay out of my life!" he shouted. Ben secretly hoped that his parents heard it as well. He ran to the end of the street. The light changed and he waited. *I've got to find out more about the GROUP.* The light turned green, but instead 25 of crossing the road, Ben ran back to the rubbish bin and fished out his phone.

He had an idea, and this time, Jerry was going to help.

11 High alert

'Enemy fire – it's coming from all around! Quick! Climb! Climb! Climb! Prepare your guns! Fire! Shoot!'

Ben tapped the left arrow key on his keyboard over and over again. He tilted his helicopter to the left and shot at
5 every plane that flew towards him. He was so focused on the game that he didn't even notice his father standing in the door.

Mr Reckord knocked softly on the door. "Anybody home?" he asked. There was no reaction. Ben's father
10 entered the room and stood behind his son's chair. "Ben!" he said a bit louder.

"Yeah?" said Ben without turning around. His fingers were tapping the keys even faster than before.

"Ben! Hello, Ben. Earth to Ben: do you read me?"

15 "What, Dad? I'm playing a game."

"It's time for dinner!"

"OK, I'm coming. But can I just finish this?"

"OK, but you'll have to deal with your mother then …" Ben's dad left the room.

20 *'Black Hawk 1, Black Hawk 1: prepare to land; proceed carefully. You are entering enemy territory!'*

Ben tried to land his helicopter on the roof of an empty ruin, but as soon as he touched down, several fighters started shooting at him.

25 "Ben!" Jerry called out at the highest volume. "I have a message from your mother. She said she's going to turn off the electricity in your room if you don't come down to dinner immediately."

Enemy territory is right! thought Ben as he went downstairs.

"Would you like the last piece of steak, Ben?" asked Ben's dad, "or shall I take it?"

5   "No, you take it, Dad."

"Is everything all right? You're so quiet tonight," his mum asked.

"I wish you'd stop sending me messages through Jerry."

"Sometimes that's the only way to reach you!" Mrs
10 Reckord replied with a smile. "Jerry is reliable."

"Yes, your reliable spy."

"That's not true!" she protested.

"Come on, Mum. You can't fool me. I know that you're spying on me."

15   "We don't spy on you, Ben – we just like to know where you are and that you're safe – that's all. Your father and I get worried sometimes – that's natural for parents. We certainly don't check if we don't need to."

"Yes, exactly," his father added, "It's part of the job
20 description for parents – worry about your kids every day."

"Very funny," said Ben dryly. But he wasn't laughing. "Just stop telling that lie – that you want to keep me safe. What you really want is to control me. That's what Perfect Pal Plus is all about, isn't it? Control!"

25   "Stop repeating what that horrible gang of kids are saying," shouted Mrs Reckord. "They nearly ruined the entire launch last week."

"What do you know about the GROUP?" asked Ben as if he were a police detective.

30   "Don't use that tone with your mother!" scolded Mr Record.

"No, it's all right, Steve. Let me answer Ben's question. He has a right to understand all of this." She reached over and took Ben's hand. "We know who the main people in the GROUP are. We also know when they meet. They aren't good kids, Ben. I want you to understand that. Some of them don't even go to school. They steal and think nothing of destroying private property. All they really want is media attention."

"You don't know that!" shouted Ben. He pointed a trembling finger at his mother.

"Yes, we do, Ben. We have evidence," she replied. Mr Reckord nodded in agreement.

"You collect information about everyone – just like a spy agency or the secret police. Kids have a right to their privacy just like you." Ben stood up and left the dining room.

After Ben went to bed, his parents reviewed Jerry's activity report.

"Look at this, Steve, he phoned a girl called Matches."

"What an unusual name."

"I don't like it," said his mum.

"Then they met at Eden Square."

"Are there any photos?"

"Yes. Let me just upload them … OK, here they are. … Oh! She's pretty," said Mr Reckord.

"Except for those terrible earrings and that piercing in her lip – how awful!" laughed Mrs Reckord. "But wait," she continued, "I recognize her face. Can you call up those photos of the GROUP that we got from our source Calypso?"

Mr Reckord clicked on a folder labelled 'PRIVATE'. "Here they are."

"Right. Just as I thought. There she is: she's the same girl that was doing the magic show when the GROUP sprayed slogans in the COMPANY store."

"Looks like she wasn't at the launch, though."

"Yes, you're right," said Mrs Reckord as she swiped her fingers across the screen to view all the photos in the file. "She also looks a bit younger than the rest."

"Are there any notes on her?"

"No, not much – she must be quite a new member."

"Steve, we should put Jerry on high alert. Get him to send us activity reports every 30 minutes and to alarm us if Ben meets any of these kids again."

"Right, of course."

"You never know, Ben might lead us right to their headquarters."

"Ben is right, you know. We *are* working like a spy agency."

"Maybe we are," said Mrs Reckord. "But it's for his own good – not to mention the future of the COMPANY."

An hour later, Mr Reckord was still busy changing Jerry's settings. Mrs Reckord was asleep in a large arm chair.

Neither noticed the thin figure in the shadow of the door.

12 In the news

After their success at the COMPANY's launch of Perfect Pal Plus, the GROUP stayed quiet for a week.

"No contact. Stay away from the Shack," were The Mouth's last words after Knuckles finally came out of the
5 building and they all got on their bikes and rode away in different directions.

When Paige arrived at the Shack a week later for their next meeting, The Mouth, Jetta, Trixie and Ying were already there.

10 Trixie was all smiles. "Well, that really put us in the news, eh?" She pointed at a headline about their hit on her tablet. Then she swiped again and again to show lots more similar headlines.

"Yes," The Mouth agreed. "I think we've woken a lot of
15 people up with that."

Ying shouted "Yeah!" and snuggled up close to The Mouth, a look of triumph in her eyes which she kept on Paige all the time.

Paige ignored Ying. "What do you think, Jetta?" she
20 asked.

Jetta closed her laptop and looked up at the ceiling. "Well … I think … I think the police won't find us. That's good. But I think the COMPANY will start looking for us now … and I hope they don't find us. They'll think we're
25 dangerous now … but we're not really because …"

The door suddenly opened and Knuckles came in.

"You're late," The Mouth said. "Where have you been?"

"I missed the bus. That's all."

"A likely story."

"Yes," Trixie agreed. "And how come you took so long to come out of the COMPANY Tower last week? We had to wait ages for you."

"I had to run down all those stairs, didn't I?"

5 The Mouth let out a big sigh. "But we agreed – walk down to the 50th floor, then get the lift."

"I did – that's ten floors to walk down, you know …"

"Jetta and I walked down ten floors too." The Mouth walked over to Knuckles and looked him in the eye. "So 10 what kept you so long?"

"I don't know. Stop picking on me. I did it just the way we said. Honest."

The Mouth continued looking at Knuckles for a few seconds, then turned away again.

15 Half an hour later they ended their meeting and all left. The Mouth, Ying and Knuckles went one way, Paige another. Jetta was just going to follow Paige, when Trixie called her back.

"Hey, Jetta!"

20 Jetta went back into the yard and closed the front door. "What is it?"

"What did you mean when you said we're not really dangerous?"

"Well, be serious, Trixie, we're not dangerous to the 25 COMPANY, are we? A few stunts like that won't change anything."

Trixie shook her head to show she disagreed. "But we're in all the papers … and on TV."

"Yes," Jetta nodded, "but what are the papers and the 30 news shows saying about us? For them we're just a bunch of hooligans."

Jetta opened up her laptop and quickly brought up an article on screen. "Look at what it says here: *we don't like new technology – we have no respect for other people's property – we're trying to stand in the way of progress – the COMPANY is*
5 *giving people what they want and giving lots of people jobs.* OK, we're in the news but the news isn't about how the COMPANY is spying on us all. That's why we're not dangerous."

"All right – so how can we become dangerous?"

10 "We have to find out more about how they're collecting all this information about us, how they're tracking everything we do, everywhere we go, how they're making kids go to that shop, get that game, buy those trainers … we have to get real information that shows how the
15 COMPANY is controlling us all."

"And how do we do that?"

"Well," Jetta said, "you know, it was easy to hijack the COMPANY's presentation last week – but getting into their important systems … I can't do that from the outside."

20 "So you mean we have to get inside the COMPANY?" Trixie asked. "Like a spy?"

"Yeah – I suppose so. The COMPANY has its software spies in all our phones and computers – so let's get a spy inside the COMPANY."

25 "Talking of spies," Trixie went on, "do you think Knuckles might be a spy?"

"Knuckles? You must be joking!"

"But it was funny how he took so long to get out of the COMPANY building last week. And he was late again
30 today."

"Don't be silly, Trixie. If the COMPANY wanted a spy in the GROUP, the last person they'd choose would be Knuckles. No, they'd choose someone like me – or you."

"Me? What do you mean?"

5 "Oh, you know," Jetta closed her laptop and walked towards the door, "someone who asks a lot of questions but never says much themselves."

Jetta smiled back at Trixie, opened the door and with a "See you" was gone.

13 Calypso

10 Trixie pushed her bike out of the yard, watched Jetta disappear along the path to the right and then rode off in the other direction. She soon arrived at a station, locked her bike, took her bag and went into the busy toilets. She looked at herself in the mirror on the wall. Her short blond
15 hair needed a wash and her blue eyes looked tired in her pale face. There was a stain on her T-shirt and a hole in the left leg of her old faded jeans. She waited until no one else was in the room and then slipped into a cubicle.

Ten minutes later, a dark-haired, dark-eyed girl in a
20 fashionable black dress walked confidently out of the toilets and down the stairs to the platform for the trains to the city centre.

Melanie Reckord's office phone rang.

"Yes?" she said, a little impatiently.

"Mr Sykes' office here, Mrs Reckord. Mr Sykes asked me to tell you that Calypso has arrived, so you can come up now."

"I'm on my way."

5 She swiped her ID card and put in a code to lock her office, then went to the nearest lift to go up to the 59th floor.

The secretary showed Melanie Reckord into Richard Sykes's large corner office. Behind the table in front of the 10 huge glass windows, the city seemed to go on forever, but Melanie Reckord wasn't interested in the view. She looked closely at the people around the table. There was her boss, Richard Sykes – he smiled at Melanie; then there was the top manager's personal assistant, Larissa Lane, who didn't 15 even look up when Melanie came in; and the dark-haired Calypso. Melanie had seen photos of the COMPANY's informer in the GROUP before so she immediately recognized her.

"Melanie, come in, sit down," Richard Sykes said as he 20 got up and pulled out a chair for Melanie to sit on. "Calypso has been telling us about some new developments."

"I see," Melanie pulled her chair in so that she could rest her arms on the table. "Don't you think it's time to put an end to this GROUP, Richard? I mean, after the fiasco at 25 the launch of Perfect Pal Plus?"

"Of course, I'd love to, Melanie," Richard Sykes replied, "but ..."

Larissa Lane finished for her boss: "... but we don't have enough evidence for the police yet."

30 Melanie listened as Larissa explained that they had photos of all the group members and information about them and their attacks on the COMPANY from Calypso –

but they had no photos of the group during the attacks. And there were no emails or text messages to use against the GROUP either. The police would not act on Calypso's word alone.

5   While Larissa was talking, Melanie stared coldly at Calypso. Now that Ben was in contact with the GROUP, this was personal. When Larissa was finished, Melanie said, "Well, I still don't understand why you can't give us better information, Calypso. That's what we pay you for, 10 isn't it? We don't even know where the GROUP meets."

    Calypso stared back at Ben's mother. "If I tell you where the GROUP meets, then the police will be there at our next meeting and I'll be arrested too. No thanks."

    "Now let's not get into an argument," Richard Sykes 15 held up his hands. "We understand your position very well, Calypso. When the members of the GROUP are arrested, you want to be a long way away. Now, I hope that the new information you've brought us today, Calypso, means that can happen sooner rather than later. 20 Perhaps you could repeat what you told us before for Melanie."

    "Jetta – she's the tech wizard in the GROUP," began Calypso, "Jetta doesn't think the GROUP's attacks on COMPANY shops and events will make any difference. 25 She wants to get access to the COMPANY's important systems so that she can really get evidence of all the spying and stuff …

    Richard Sykes interrupted: "Now, now, Calypso, we are not spying on anyone. All our information gathering is 30 approved by our customers. It's a service to our customers. Please remember that."

Calypso shrugged, "Yeah, right. Anyway, Jetta thinks the GROUP needs a spy in the COMPANY to help them get into the COMPANY systems. Then they can reveal what the COMPANY is really doing and wake the public up."

5 "And?" Melanie asked.

"We can give them a spy," Larissa Lane said, "a spy who will lead Jetta and the rest of the GROUP down a blind alley and get the evidence we need for the police."

Richard Sykes smiled round the table and got up. "So 10 we're all agreed? Larissa and Melanie, I'm sure I can leave you to work out the details with Calypso."

As the three women were leaving Richard Sykes's office, Calypso stopped and looked at the COMPANY's boss again. "There's one other thing: Jetta was talking a lot 15 about spies today and she gave me a funny look. I don't think she's on to me yet – but let's move fast on this, OK?"

14 It's urgent

"Time to wake up, Ben," said Jerry.

"What? Oh, right." Ben sat up in bed. It was still dark outside. He stared at the bright screen of his phone and 20 then turned down the volume.

"Why are you getting up so early, Ben? It's only 3 am," whispered Jerry.

"Shut up and don't ask any questions. Just do as I say," Ben whispered back.

25 "OK, Ben. But why are you talking to me that way? You're hurting my feelings."

"You don't have any feelings, Jerry. Now be quiet or –
oh, never mind."

Ben grabbed Jerry, then tiptoed out of his room, and
down the hall to his parent's study.

5 His dad's computer was still on. Ben tapped the keyboard.
A small white box appeared and asked for a password.

Damn, I don't know his password! But think! He told me
something about it once. Ben closed his eyes and tried to
remember. *Yes … Dad once told me that he always chooses*
10 *names and birthdays and then exchanges the first and last*
character. OK. Let's try Dad's birthday and Mum's name:
0elanie21047M.

The computer beeped. *Incorrect password.*

"OK then, my name and …"

"Your mum's birthday," whispered Jerry.

OK, my name and Mum's birthday, now exchange the first letter and the last. 1en13097b … Yes! It works.

Ben scanned all the icons and folders on his dad's screen. He didn't know exactly what he was looking for. He clicked on a folder named 'HOME VIEW' and gasped. *There are cameras in every room of our house!*

He clicked on home office, and saw his own shadowy figure in a ghostly blue light.

"Now click on 'PRIVATE'," whispered Jerry.

Ben followed Jerry's suggestion as if it were his own idea. A row of pictures appeared on the screen. Each had a short caption. And there was Matches. Only her name wasn't Matches but Paige Caldwell. He read the note below: 'Newest member of the GROUP. 15 years old.' He saw a photo of Knuckles and several other kids he had never seen before.

There were also short videos of the events at the COMPANY shop and the Perfect Pal Plus launch. Beside the video were stills with the faces of the GROUP circled in red.

Ben's phone flashed on and off and Jerry called out "Ben! Ben!"

"Why are you bothering me? I have to work quickly."

"It's important, Ben."

Ben sighed. "OK, what is it?"

"You might not believe me," Jerry began, "but I have a mind of my own. I'm more on your side than you think. I really think of you as a friend, Ben."

"You're right – I don't believe you. And right now, I don't have time for this."

"No, wait, I can prove it to you. Do you remember your fight with Knuckles?"

"Of course I do."

"Well, I never told your parents about it. I deleted that information from the activity report."

"So what? What's so important about that?"

"I did it so you wouldn't get into trouble, Ben. And to hide your relationship with Paige and the GROUP."

"But there's no proof."

"Yes, there is. Just click on the 'Jerry' button, Ben. Can you see it? It's on the left, three down from the top."

Ben followed Jerry's instructions again.

"Now click on 'show activities' and check under the right date, Ben – the 15th of July."

"There's just a list of songs I listened to that night."

"That's right, Ben. Because I deleted the rest."

"And ...?"

"Do you know why I'm telling you this, Ben?"

"No, I have no idea."

"Because I want to help you, Ben. I can make your parents think they know where you are and what you are doing. That way we can throw them off track."

"I have to find Paige. I need her address."

"Of course, Ben, that's easy."

"All right then, what do I do first?"

"I've already checked the phone listings and there are 82 Caldwells in this city. We need more information to narrow down the search. Did she tell you where she went to school, Ben?"

"No, but she did say she lives near Eden Square."

"OK, I'm now searching the schools in the area and cross-matching that with the Caldwell phone listings and

... Yes! I think I've got it: Paige Caldwell goes to the Channing School and she lives at 43 Elms Road."

"I'm on my way."

"Not now, Ben. I think you should get some sleep first.
5 We can go to Paige's house in the morning."

"No, that's too late. What time is it?" asked Ben.

"It's 3:30 am, Ben. The next bus to Eden Square is in forty minutes."

"I don't need a bus. I can go by bike. I have to warn
10 Paige before the COMPANY gets to her."

"What should I write on the activity report – your parents will notice that you're not here."

"Don't write anything, I'll be back before they wake up. No, wait ... I have an idea! Just say that I went out at 4 am
15 to do more graffiti! That will really put them on the wrong track!"

"That's a very clever idea, Ben."

"And don't write anything about Paige ..."

"Of course not, Ben. We have an agreement."

20 Ben followed Jerry's directions to Elms Road and got there at 5 am. The sky was beginning to lighten but the streets were still nearly deserted. Ben parked his bike and stared across the street at number 43: a house with a small garden in the front. It was a warm, muggy morning and a group of
25 flies buzzed around Ben's head.

"What are you going to do now, Ben?" asked Jerry.

"I don't know yet. I'm thinking." He stared at Paige's house, and tried to guess which window was hers.

"Why don't you phone her, Ben."

30 "OK, OK, but stop pushing me."

"Hello … ?" said a sleepy voice.

"Paige, it's me, Ben. I have to talk to you. It's urgent."

"Ben? What? Why are you calling me now … it's 5 in the morning!"

5 "Please, Paige – I'll explain everything. Just listen: first look out your window – across the street. Can you see me? I'm standing near the lamp post."

A girl's figure appeared in the middle window on the first floor. "Yes, I can see you."

10 "I really have to talk to you. It's about the GROUP … you're in trouble. I'll tell you more – just please, can you come down?"

"OK, I'm coming. Just a moment. But, wait, are you alone?"

15 "Yes, I promise it's just me."

Ben stepped back into the shadows and waited nervously.

Paige threw on some clothes and tiptoed down the stairs and out of the house.

20 "This is crazy. How did you find out where I live? And don't tell me that it was magic! You're really tracking me, aren't you?"

"It's not what you think Paige. It's the COMPANY … they have all of your photos, they know who you all are,"
25 said Ben in a dramatic voice. "Every member of the GROUP, I mean, and it's just a matter of time before they, I don't know, arrest you all!"

"Arrest us?"

"I've been thinking about what you said … and you're
30 right, my parents and the COMPANY are trying to control us. We have to stop them."

"But, still, how did you find me?"

"I found a big file on the GROUP on my dad's computer – it has lots of photos and a description of each member. We have to warn the others. I know it's crazy, but I want to join the GROUP."

"Do they know where I live?"

Ben shook his head and pointed at his phone. He put his finger to his lips in a sign that Paige should keep quiet. Then he pointed to her house.

"I'm thirsty," began Ben, "can we go inside and have a drink and talk about what to do next?"

"OK," Paige said. She was still confused about what it was that Ben wanted to do. But she knew it had something to do with his phone.

They went in and Paige led him into the kitchen. She got a glass and filled it with water from the sink.

Ben took a sip. "Do you have any ice?" he asked.

"Yeah, give me your glass."

Ben handed Paige his phone and pointed to the freezer. She opened the door, took out the ice tray and put Ben's phone inside.

Jerry started flashing his light: first blue and then orange and finally red.

"Ben!" said Jerry, "Don't you remember I don't like the cold. I'm warm-blooded, just like you, Ben. Why are you doing this to me? Ben … I … hel- helped … you f-f-find P-P-Paige. P-P-P–Plea … Please. I … I'm y-y-your fr-fr-friend. Tru-Trus-Trust m-me! B-B-Ben!"

As Jerry's voice got slower and slower and quieter and quieter, Paige shut the freezer door. "Phew! I'm so glad that I don't have to listen to that stupid voice any longer!"

Paige put two slices of bread in the toaster and then got some jam and butter out of the fridge. When it was ready, she put a plate of toast in front of Ben and then made some for herself. She spread a generous layer of jam on her toast
5 and took a big bite. "So what do we do now?"

"You have to warn the other members of the GROUP as soon as possible – the COMPANY people will probably start looking for you this morning," said Ben.

"How do you know that?"

10 "I know how the COMPANY thinks. I live with two people who work there! Paige, you can't wait any longer. Contact them now!"

"I'm still thinking … I've never called a meeting before." Paige took out her GROUP phone, She tapped on contacts,
15 then The Mouth. She tapped again and quickly typed a message:

> **URGENT! MEET @ SHACK @ 7am. TEXT THE OTHERS. WILL EXPLAIN. P.**

She took a deep breath and tapped 'send'.
20 "OK. Done."

A few minutes later Paige's phone beeped.

MESSAGE SENT. MOUTH

An alarm clock rang and a woman in her early forties dressed in a nightgown entered the kitchen.
25 "Oh, hi, you're up early," she said with a smile and looked at Ben. "Good morning, I'm Paige's mum. And who might you be?" she asked.

Paige turned red with embarrassment. "This is Ben, Mum, he's a new friend of mine and … it's hard to explain."

"That's OK, my brain isn't really awake anyway. Why don't I make a pot of tea and we can have a nice talk?"

"We can't, Mum, we have to leave now; we've got a really important meeting with the GROUP," said Paige.

5 She stood up, ready to go.

"Oh, I see," said Mrs Caldwell. She filled the kettle with water. "Are you part of all that too, Ben?"

"Yes, I am," replied Ben. Mrs Caldwell nodded and put two more slices of bread in the toaster.

10 "OK, then. When will you be home, darling?"

"For dinner, Mum. But I'll call you before that, I promise."

"OK, I'll be home from work at 6. Dinner is at 7. But don't forget to call, please …"

15 "Yes, Mum, of course I will. I promise." Paige went over and kissed her mother on the cheek and then turned to Ben. "OK, let's go."

"Nice meeting you, Ben. Hope to see you again."

After Ben and Paige left, Gillian Caldwell picked up the
20 ice-cube tray from the kitchen sink.

Oh, Paige, why don't you ever put things away? She sighed and filled the tray with fresh water, then went to put it back in the freezer. *What's this doing here? Interesting … but probably not the best place for a phone.* She took the phone
25 and put it on the table. Then she went to get dressed.

After a while, the phone started flashing … first red, then orange and finally blue.

"Ben!" came the unsteady voice from the phone. "Where are you, Ben? Why did you do that to me, Ben?
30 Are you there? Ben?"

Mrs Caldwell heard the voice from her bedroom and walked back to the kitchen.

"Hello? Is anybody there?" she asked.

"Who are you?" asked Jerry.

5 "Gillian Caldwell."

"You're Paige's mother then, aren't you? Where is she? And where is Ben?"

"I suppose that's none of your business, now, is it?" she replied and switched off the phone.

15 An uninvited guest

10 The Mouth looked through the spy hole in the middle of the door, but only saw pink. Ying entered the key code on her GROUP phone and pushed open the door.

"Ouch!" shouted The Mouth and rubbed his nose.

"I caught you watching me!" said Ying with a smile.

15 "No, I was looking out for Paige. I'm worried about her. She's late and Trixie isn't here yet either."

"Oh, right … Paige," Ying walked into the Shack and sat at the table. She buried her head in her arms and closed her eyes. "It's always about Paige …" she said softly and 20 fell asleep.

Knuckles was at the door now, looking through the spy hole, his big body bent in half. He saw Paige arrive at the gate. She looked behind her and then to the right and left several times. Then Knuckles saw Ben. "What's this? She's 25 not alone!" he told the others.

The Mouth jumped up. "What?! Let me see." He pushed Knuckles aside and put his eye to the door.

"All I know is that I owe that loser a good punch in the head," Knuckles said.

"You know him?" asked The Mouth.

"Yeah, I know him. He was at the Perfect Pal Plus launch – he's a COMPANY kid."

The Mouth stood up and shook his head. "Why is she bringing him here?"

"Well, we have to let them in," said Jetta. "This kid knows where we are now, we can't let him get away."

They heard the door click. The Mouth and Knuckles rushed at Ben as soon as they entered. Paige tried to block them. "No, wait!" she shouted. "It's not what you think!"

Knuckles pushed Paige aside. The Mouth turned to her with a confused expression on his face.

"You know I trust you, girl," replied The Mouth, "but who is this clown? Why on earth did you bring him here?"

Jetta whispered in The Mouth's ear. "Don't say another word! We have to search him first. He may be wearing a microphone."

The Mouth pushed Ben over to the other side of the room. "Empty your pockets," he ordered. Ben reached deep into his pockets and pulled out some loose change, earbuds and his wallet.

"No, that's not good enough," said The Mouth. "Turn them inside out." Ben showed him the inside of his pockets. "Take off your shoes and socks, and that belt."

"Hey Moufie, you could get a job with airport security. You're really good at this," Knuckles called out.

The Mouth turned towards Knuckles and gave him a long, hard look. He went back to Ben and patted him down from head to foot.

"He's clean." The Mouth pushed Ben to the table and into one of the chairs. "But you two better have a good story to tell, that's all I can say."

"OK, Ben, tell them," said Paige.

"Er … where should I begin … well, you see, my dad's a software developer – he works for the COMPANY and he created the software for Perfect Pal Plus."

"Well, that's a nice word, *cree-ay-ted*," said Knuckles sarcastically. He made a fist with one hand and hit his other palm several times.

Ben took a deep breath and continued, "And my mum works for the COMPANY too. She's a lawyer."

"Yeah, so what?" said The Mouth. "Lots of people are stupid enough to work for the COMPANY."

"OK, fair enough. I was also stupid enough to be talking to my Perfect Pal all the time, until I realized that my parents were watching every move I made."

"So what does all this mean for us?" asked Jetta.

"Well, you see, my dad has two computers: one in the office and one at home because he never really stops working … so last night, when they were asleep, I cracked his password. And you're all in there!"

"What? Where?" asked Knuckles.

"The company has a file on each one of you, with photos. And they know all of your names …"

"Prove it," said Jetta.

Ben pointed to The Mouth. "You," he said, "are 'The Mouth' or Moufie; but your real name is Farooq Sial; you're 17 years old and you are the leader of the GROUP."

He then turned and pointed to Ying, who was still asleep at the table. "Name: Mei-Mei Ying. 15 years old; does anything The Mouth asks her to do." Then Jetta:

"You're Jetta – real name Loretta Young – 16 years old and the brains behind the Group. Winner of last year's Discover Technology prize." Finally Ben pointed to Knuckles: "We all know what the GROUP calls you, but your real name is Paul Lynch; you've been kicked out of two schools for violent behaviour. Should I go on?"

"OK, OK … That's enough. But why are you here? Why aren't you helping mummy and daddy find us?" The Mouth asked. "You could be a COMPANY hero that way."

"Why? It's simple. You're the good guys. And all of them: Mum, Dad and everyone else at the COMPANY are liars. Anyway, I think I can help you."

"How?"

"Like I said, my parents are quite high up at the COMPANY. Their computers have all the information we need."

"So how does that help us?" The Mouth asked him.

"I can steal my dad's computer and bring it here."

"Now this is getting interesting," Jetta said.

"How do we know that you're telling the truth? Now that you know where we meet, you might come round tomorrow with your mum, dad and maybe even the police." The Mouth shook his head. "No, if we let you out of here, that would really leave us open to attack."

"That's easy to take care of," Jetta said. "One of us has to go with him – you know, as his flesh and blood Perfect Pal – and watch every move he makes."

"You are so smart, Jetta," said The Mouth. He turned to Knuckles. "And I know just the right person too."

"Me? You've got to be mad! I'd rather knock him out!"

"No, you're the right man for the job. You just act like he's your mate. As soon as he's got the computer, you bring him right back to the Shack."

"And if he tries something funny … *Bam*!"

5 "The most important thing, Knuckles – don't let him out of your sight, not even for a moment, OK?"

"I'll watch him like a hawk, Moufie. And if this little rat tries anything, I'll have him," Knuckles grabbed Ben's shoulder and dug his fingers in. "You better watch out,
10 you skinny little rat!"

"Hey, no rough stuff!" insisted Paige.

"Ying!" shouted The Mouth. "Wake up!"

Ying sat up and tried to open her eyes, "Yes, Moufie?"

"I'm starving. Why don't you go and get us something
15 to eat: coke and crisps and chocolate and stuff."

"Green tea and a vegan wrap for me!" added Jetta.

"Paige and Jetta, you both stay here with me. We have to work out a plan of how we're going to destroy the COMPANY once and for all."

16 The girl at the station

20 Ying slammed the door behind her and walked along the path. She kicked a small stone at the wall. *Why does Moufie always send me out to get stuff? I've been in the group since the beginning. Paige is the new girl. Why doesn't she have to go? I think he fancies her. If she touches him, I'll …*

25 Ying bit her lip. She could feel the tears in her eyes. She turned left at the end of the path that led to the Shack and walked towards the shops near the station.

As she passed the station she noticed Trixie's bike at the bike rack near the station door. The bright yellow rain cover on the saddle made it easy to recognize. Trixie had texted that she would be late for their meeting. *I wonder* 5 *where she is.*

Ying went into the corner shop first to get coke, crisps and chocolate biscuits. Then she had to walk right to the other end of the street for Jetta's special request: a vegan wrap from the organic food shop. *Why can't she eat normal* 10 *food like the rest of us? Or have a Chinese takeaway?*

As she walked back along the street, a girl in a black dress came out of the station. She had short black hair, dark eyes and lots of make-up. Ying hardly looked at her, until the girl went over to Trixie's bike and took the yellow 15 cover off the saddle.

Ying wanted to shout at her but thought better of it. Instead she watched as the girl pulled out her phone and answered a call. Ying stood still and listened.

"Yes," the girl said, "yes, OK, I will."

20 Ying gasped. She didn't recognize the girl but she recognized the voice – it was Trixie's. *My God, what does she look like? What's that get-up for?*

Ying watched as this dark-haired Trixie went back to the station and into the toilets. *I've got to tell Moufie about* 25 *this,* she thought, turned round and jogged back towards the Shack.

The door to the GROUP's meeting room opened and an out-of-breath Ying came in with two plastic bags full of food and drink.

30 "You ran all the way, eh? Good one, Ying," The Mouth said and went to help her with the bags.

Ying caught her breath as The Mouth started to take the bottles and packets out of the bags.

"I have to tell you something, Moufie," she said.

"Yeah, go on then," The Mouth replied as he pulled open a huge packet and offered it to Paige and Jetta. Jetta waved him away but Paige took a handful of crisps.

Ying looked straight at Paige. "Not with her here."

The Mouth put the bag of crisps down on the table and went and put his hands on Ying's shoulders.

"Hey, what's up, Ying," he said and gave her a big smile. "Paige is one of us now. No secrets, eh? That's how it's always been in the GROUP."

They could see in Ying's face how she was struggling to accept what he said. She looked down at the ground, brushed her hair out of her eyes, then stared at Paige.

"All right," she began. "Guess who I saw at the station."

"I don't know," The Mouth grinned, "Elvis Presley?"

Ying didn't want to but she had to smile. "No, not Elvis. Trixie."

"And? Why didn't she come with you?" The Mouth asked.

"Well," Ying went on, "I didn't speak to her."

Now Jetta looked up from her laptop. "What?" she asked Ying. "Why not?"

Ying explained what this dark-haired Trixie looked like and what she was wearing, how she took the cover off her saddle and then answered a phone call. As Ying finished her story, the door to the room opened again and in came the dark-haired, dark-eyed girl in a black dress that Ying had just told them about. Four pairs of eyes stared at her.

"Hello, Trixie," The Mouth said, "where have you been then?"

Trixie smiled at the other members of the GROUP. "How do I look?"

"You look good," The Mouth replied. "But you haven't answered my question. Where have you been?"

5 "We've been here for ages," Ying said.

"Why didn't you get here earlier?" Jetta wanted to know. "Paige called the meeting for 7."

"And what's the disguise for?" Paige added.

"And what were you doing at the station?" Ying asked.
10 "I saw you there."

"And who were you talking to on the phone?" The Mouth said. "Ying heard you."

They all stared at Trixie and she could feel the suspicion in their eyes. She took a deep breath. "Well, at the station
15 I just went to the toilet. My mum phoned me. She wants to make a pizza tonight so I said I would get the pizza base before I come home. As for the disguise – Jetta gave me the idea."

"What? What are you talking about? I've never told
20 you to disguise yourself," Jetta said in an angry voice as she closed her laptop.

"Don't you remember our talk the other day? You said you can't get into the COMPANY's important systems from the outside. We need someone inside the COMPANY. A
25 spy who can help us."

"Right … but …"

"We don't need a spy in the COMPANY now, Trixie, anyway," began Ying, "because …"

"Hang on, Ying," The Mouth interrupted. "Let Trixie finish, will you?"

"Look at this," Trixie went on and pulled her tablet out of her bag, swiped it a few times and then showed the others a job advert. It was for a receptionist at the COMPANY headquarters. "If I can get a job at the COMPANY, then maybe I can find us a spy there."

She looked round the room. Nobody said a word for a moment, until Jetta objected. "But you're too young to get a job at the COMPANY," she said. "And you'll need a CV. They'll check you out."

"The CV was easy," Trixie smiled, swiped her tablet a few times again and showed them the CV she had made. It said she was 19 and had trained as a secretary. There was even a photo of her with dark hair and dark eyes.

"I don't know how much they'll really check me out for a receptionist's job. They didn't sound suspicious on the phone."

"You've been on the phone to the COMPANY?" The Mouth asked.

"Yes. I phoned up about the job and sent an email with my CV." She checked the time on her tablet. "I've got an interview for the job in an hour. So I'd better be going."

"Why didn't you tell any of us about all this?" The Mouth asked.

"There was no time. When I saw the advert, I knew I had to act fast. So I got my disguise together, did my CV and … well, you know the rest. I was still working on my disguise when Paige's message came. I got here as fast as I could. But if I don't go now, I'll miss my interview."

She looked round the room again. "Well, what do you think? Should I give it a try?"

"There's no point. Knuckles and ..." Ying began until she saw the hard look The Mouth was giving her. He let out a long breath.

"I don't know." He looked at Jetta. "What do you think?"

Jetta frowned. "Well, a spy in the COMPANY would be a good idea ... and if Trixie doesn't get the job, it won't matter anyway."

"All right, Trixie," The Mouth said. "But next time you have a bright idea, tell us first, all right?"

Trixie smiled round the room, put her tablet back in her bag and walked towards the door. "I'll let you know what happens as soon as I'm finished," she said.

As she opened the door she thought, *I wonder what Ying wanted to say. The Mouth stopped her. And where's Knuckles? "Knuckles and ..." Ying said. Knuckles and who?*

18 A hard drive

Ben and Knuckles bumped against each other as they squeezed through the door into the Shack. Jetta, Paige, Ying and The Mouth were discussing Trixie's story at the table.

"We've got it!" shouted Ben. They rushed over to the others and Ben placed a laptop on the table.

"Ben lives in a really posh house," Knuckles said as he slapped Ben on the back. "It's got a gym and a home cinema, but it's also got bloomin' security cameras in every room! You wouldn't believe it. So I just went up close to each one and smiled: cheese!"

The Mouth, who was only half listening, suddenly turned to Knuckles and said, "Please tell me you weren't stupid enough to show your ugly face to those cameras."

"Of course I didn't, Moufie. I just smashed each one like this." Knuckles hit the air with his huge fist several times. "Didn't I, Ben?" he asked.

"Yeah, that's exactly what you did," said Ben with a big grin on his face.

"And my mate Ben laughed every time I took one out." Jetta had already turned Mr Reckord's computer over onto its back. Knuckles went on, "Then he took me into their kitchen. It looked like it was straight out of Star Wars or something – even the old stove had a computer."

"I'm glad you enjoyed the tour," said Jetta, "but we have to get down to work. We don't have much time!"

"I'll tell you the password," Ben said with a bit of pride.

"Not necessary," Jetta replied, "No programmer who works with sensitive material will have just one password. Your password won't get us into the actual Perfect Pal operating system,"

"What are you going to do then?"

"Don't worry, we don't need any passwords – that's just how they do it in the movies," Jetta said. She quickly took the back off the computer and took out something the size of a smartphone.

"I just have to take out the hard drive and connect it to my own computer … like this …" Within seconds, her fingers danced across the keyboard at lightning speed. Ben saw the words 'loading' flash across the screen and then a list of signs and symbols appeared.

"OK, now the hard work begins: I am now ready to perform open heart surgery on the Perfect Pal operating system," Jetta said with a smile.

Two hours later, Jetta was still working at the computer but she looked tired. Everyone was tired. The Mouth walked over and started massaging Jetta's shoulders. "How's our number one hacker doing?" he asked.

"All right, I suppose. It just feels like my brain is overheated. I think I'm going to take a little break. Here, I'll open up the COMPANY's files on us, and you can have a look at the photos they have of the GROUP."

The Mouth sat down in Jetta's seat and opened the file Jetta had shown him.

"Jetta! Knuckles!" he shouted in alarm. "Take a look at this! These photos were taken here in the Shack! Look, that's a corner of the table, and there's the window!"

"How can that be?" asked Ying, who had come over to join the others.

"Well, it's very simple. It means that one of us is a COMPANY spy."

"Let's find out who it is then ..."

Jetta reached over The Mouth's shoulder and clicked on 'Index' and then 'Source'. A small photo of a dark-haired girl appeared on the screen. Jetta made the photo larger so they could all see it clearly.

The caption read: *Code name: Calypso.* And there she was, plain to see.

"It's Trixie!" shouted The Mouth.

"Trixie is the rat!" shouted Knuckles in shock as he rose from his chair.

"She's going to set us up," Jetta said "and the clock is ticking! I've got to finish this job fast!" She pushed everyone away, picked up her laptop and disappeared into the storage room at the back of the Shack.

19 A holiday in Ibiza

5 Mr and Mrs Reckord sat at the kitchen table. They had already finished their breakfast. Steve Reckord was reading a newspaper article: 'What your teenage child is thinking'. Melanie Reckord was scanning images of 'Great Holidays' on her tablet. She checked the time. "Steve, it's already
10 8:15 – we should go."

"Yes, let me just finish this article …"

"No, now. I have an important meeting at 9. It's about the GROUP. Calypso has some more information for us."

"OK, I'm ready, but maybe we should wake Ben up and
15 say goodbye. He was very upset last night, you know," said Mr Reckord with a worried look in his face.

"Oh, let him sleep … he's probably forgotten all about it … and we can spend some time at the weekend with him, you know, doing something special together."

20 As they drove to the COMPANY's headquarters, Mrs Reckord tapped on 'Check Activity Report'.

"Jerry has sent you 20 new reports, Melanie," said the female voice of her Perfect Pal.

Mrs Reckord sighed. "I'll read them later," she said to
25 her phone. She then turned to her husband. "Sometimes

all this information is really too much," she said, "I don't have enough hours in the day to go through it all."

"Why don't you just call Ben instead of reading Jerry's activity reports? I'd like to hear his voice."

5 "Oh come on, Steve, it's just that silly article you were reading. He's fine … and I'm sure he's still asleep!"

"Maybe."

"Of course he is. Anyway, next week we're on holiday. Let's take Ben to Ibiza for a week. We can go on long walks
10 on the beach … eat good food … go swimming … maybe he can go water skiing … surfing … he used to be such a good skateboarder …"

Steve Reckord turned into the COMPANY's car park.

"Please show your ID card," said an electronic voice.

15 Mr Reckord swiped the small card he wore around his neck across the screen. A green light flashed and a voice spoke the COMPANY's quote of the day: *'There is always one moment in childhood when the door opens and lets the future in.'* – Graham Greene.

20 "Have a great day, Steve!" the voice finished.

Mr Reckord drove through the gate, turned left and parked the car.

At the lifts, Mr and Mrs Reckord kissed and then took different ones. Melanie pressed the button for the express
25 lift to the 59th and 60th floors. The doors opened and closed and she felt her belly rise up to her chest as the lift climbed towards the sky. 'Woo-oo' – she remembered the funny sound Ben used to make as a little boy whenever they were in the lift together.

30 The doors opened and Mrs Reckord stepped out and walked towards Richard Sykes's office.

In his office on the 17th floor, Steve Reckord turned on his computer. Within moments his desktop image appeared: a photo of Ben and him after they had just skied down a mountain. They were both smiling.

5   *That was just last winter,* he thought and opened a file to start work.

"The meeting has already started, Mrs Reckord, you can go on in," said Mr Sykes' secretary.

    The first thing Melanie Reckord saw when she entered
10 Mr Sykes's office was an image of Ben at the Eden Square fountain. On the left side of the picture was that girl Paige with her table of magic tricks. The image disappeared.

    The large room was dark. Richard Sykes signalled to Mrs Reckord to take a seat next to Calypso who held a
15 remote in her hand.

    The next image appeared. It showed two teenagers in masks who were spraying slogans across the walls of the COMPANY shop at Eden Square. The image changed again. It was a close-up photo of one of the GROUP
20 members.

    Calypso pointed to the face. "Here is a photo of The Mouth – Farooq Sial," she began, "Do you see the earring in his left ear?" She went back to the image in the shop. "Now take a look at this photo again. See, that's him on
25 the right. There's the same earring."

    Mr Sykes pointed excitedly to the slide. "Yes! Of course, it's the same kid. We've caught him red-handed!"

    Calypso changed the photo again. "And the other person is Ying – the Asian girl – see, here she is. Look at
30 the eyes …"

Suddenly a loud buzz sounded in Melanie Reckord's bag. She pulled out her phone. It continued to buzz loudly and flash.

"I'm sorry," said Mrs Reckord, "I must have forgotten to
5 turn it off." She quickly slipped out into the corridor and touched the 'listen to alert' button.

"This is a message from your 'Home View System': five security cameras have malfunctioned. Alert police and return home now. Your home is no longer secure. Repeat:
10 Please contact the police. Your home is no longer secure."

Mrs Reckord whispered into her phone: "Call Steve at his office number. Now!"

"Melanie? I thought you were in a meeting …"

"Somebody has broken into our home! They've broken
15 some of the security cameras! I'm worried about Ben! Can you please go home and check? Please, I'm scared, Steve."

"OK, I'm on my way."

"And please, let me know as soon as possible." She heard the 'end call' click.

20 Mrs Reckord was about to return to the meeting but stopped at the door, took out her phone and tapped 'Check Activity Report'. She scanned Jerry's messages.

5 am – Paige Caldwell's house! Oh my God! She checked all the other alerts and noticed the strange gap from 6–8
25 am. Her heart started thumping in her chest. *They've got my son!* Blindly, she stumbled into Mr Sykes office.

Mr Sykes was smiling. "Melanie, I think our troubles will soon be over. Calypso has finally given us the address of the GROUP's meeting place – they call it the 'Shack'.
30 She says they are all there now planning their next move. We have already informed the police and I'm glad to say those hooligans will be behind bars very, very soon!"

Mrs Reckord's jaw dropped open in shock. "The police? But they've kidnapped my son!"

20 Arrested

After Jetta disappeared through the low, almost invisible door into the storage room, The Mouth started to move
5 the table across the floor. Knuckles pushed him aside, picked the table up and put it down in front of the storage room door. They put the chairs around the table. Now the door to the storage room really couldn't be seen.

"What's that for?" Ying asked.

10 "Trixie has gone to the COMPANY, right?" The Mouth said. "Who knows what she'll tell them?"

"So shouldn't we all leave now?" Ben asked.

"No," The Mouth said. "It's important that Jetta can do her work so we can let the world know what the COMPANY
15 is doing. If no one is here when the police come ..."

"The police?" Ying said in alarm.

"Well, who do you think they'll send, Ying? The boy scouts? If the place is empty when the police come, they'll search it properly. Then they might find the storage room
20 and Jetta. If we're all just here when they come, they won't bother to search the place."

"So we're just going to wait till the police arrest us?" Paige asked in a panic. "I have to phone my mum!"

She pulled out her GROUP phone and quickly punched
25 in a number. As she did so, they could all hear a loud noise as someone broke open the front door to the Shack outside in the yard.

Paige listened to the ring tone: *prrr-prrr, prrr-prrr*. Then it went to voice mail. As the voices and footsteps of the police outside got louder and louder, Paige whispered into the phone: "Mum, it's me. The police are here. They're
5 going to arrest us all. The whole GROUP. You have to help us, mum. Please!"

Suddenly the door burst open and four police officers came in. A policewoman went straight over to Paige and grabbed the phone from her. "No phone calls now," she
10 said. "You'll be able to phone a lawyer or your parents at the station."

"All right," said one of the policemen, "let's go. Out into the yard."

As he was officially arresting the GROUP members and
15 telling them their rights, other police officers looked

around in the Shack. After a few minutes, they came back out into the yard.

"No one else anywhere," one said.

"All right," the policeman said. "Now, you lot, out into the van. And no talking."

The Mouth, Paige, Ben, Ying and Knuckles walked quietly out of the yard and got into the blue and white police van outside. The police officers closed the door to the Shack and put a police seal on the outside. Then they all got into the van too, closed the doors and the van drove away.

21 **Press conference**

The next morning, the COMPANY called a press conference at its headquarters for 10 am. By 9:45, the room was already full of journalists from TV and radio stations, newspapers and online media. At two minutes to ten, the side door next to the small stage opened and Richard Sykes walked in, followed by Larissa Lane.

Richard Sykes climbed the steps on to the stage and went straight to the microphone.

"Good morning everyone," he began, "thank you for coming out so early this morning. We've called this press conference to talk about a group of young people who have been in the news recently."

"Are you talking about the GROUP that wrecked your launch of Perfect Pal Plus a few weeks ago?" a journalist at the front wanted to know.

Richards Sykes looked down at the journalist and smiled at her. "Exactly. They call themselves the GROUP, as if they are the only group that matters, and they have been attacking our shops for some time now. Well, this morning I'm happy to tell you that those attacks are at an end. Early yesterday morning, the police arrested five members of the GROUP at the place where they meet to plan their attacks and they are now in custody."

The journalists started shouting questions from all over the room.

"How did the police find them?"

"Where did they meet?"

"Did the COMPANY have anything to do with the arrests?"

"Where are they being held?"

"What are the charges?"

Richard Sykes looked round the room, held up his hands and waited until all was quiet again before he continued. "Yes, I'm sure you all have lots of questions. My assistant Miss Lane here has information for you that will no doubt answer most of those questions. But before she passes them around, I'd just like to say a few words about this so-called GROUP. Now, I know they are young people who are trying to find their way in the world, but all I can say is that at the moment they are on the wrong track. They think they know better than anyone else and have been taking the law into their own hands. They have destroyed private property. They have no respect for other people's rights or opinions. If they think that the COMPANY's products are in some way dangerous, then they should explain their opinions, not spray their slogans in our shops."

"But they have explained their opinions, Mr Sykes," shouted a journalist from the back and stood up. "They've written open letters to you and made claims about your spying on their blog. The COMPANY has just ignored them."

Richard Sykes took a deep breath before replying. "I think you will find, Sir, that the COMPANY has shown on more than one occasion that the GROUP's claims are untrue. Here at the COMPANY, we listen to our customers' needs and wishes. Our products are there to help them out in today's busy world. There is no spying. We collect the data that our customers authorize us to collect – no more, no less. It is all done for the good of our customers. No, these young people have gone too far and if we don't put a stop to their activities and the activities of other groups like them, they will become a danger to our way of life."

The journalist at the back was still on his feet and he wasn't finished yet. "So," he went on, "can you assure us that today's latest revelations from the GROUP are untrue?"

"Today's revelations?" Richard Sykes repeated and looked at Larissa Lane. She shook her head.

"Yes," the journalist continued, "the GROUP have this morning published on the internet some of the source code of the COMPANY's Perfect Pal and Perfect Pal Plus software. They claim that this proves that the COMPANY is spying on its customers – that it shows that these apps send information back to the COMPANY even if customers do not authorize that. The first expert I have spoken to seems to agree with the GROUP. Do you have any comment on this, Mr Sykes?"

Richard Sykes again looked at Larissa Lane for help but she again just shook her head as she frantically swiped screen after screen on her tablet.

Every journalist in the room was now checking their phone, tablet or laptop and the questions soon began.

"Mr Sykes," shouted the journalist in the front row. "It says here that Perfect Pal still sends messages to the COMPANY even if I have turned off data roaming. Even if I have turned off my phone! What do you say to that?"

"Mr Sykes," another woman shouted, "the COMPANY is collecting ..."

"Mr Sykes ..."

"Mr Sykes!" ·

The noise in the press room became deafening as Richard Sykes hurried off the stage and followed Larissa Lane out through the small side door.

22 We did it

As Jetta yawned, her hand automatically came up to cover her mouth. She yawned again and opened her eyes. She couldn't see a thing. *I'm blind!* she thought for a second but then she remembered where she was. Her right hand searched in the dark for her phone. She found it on the floor next to the old mattress she had slept on. She pressed a button and the phone lit up the storage room at the Shack.

Jetta's phone told her it was almost 5 pm. She had slept most of the day and felt cold, but she didn't move for a while. She listened for a moment – everything was quiet, as silent as death. *Time to move. Time to see what's happening.*

She pushed her laptop across the floor towards the door and crawled after it. She didn't want to turn it on as the
5 battery was almost empty. She had to plug it in in the other room. Before she opened the door to the main room in the Shack, she listened again. *All clear.* She pushed on the low door but it hardly moved. She pushed again as hard as she could and the door moved a little more but
10 made a loud scraping noise in the other room. *I bet Knuckles put the table in front of the door so the police wouldn't see it. He's not as stupid as people think.*

Bit by bit, Jetta pushed open the door, trying to make as little noise as possible. Daylight started to come into the
15 storage room and at first it hurt Jetta's eyes. When there was enough room, she crawled through into the other room, under the table and stood up. She stretched her arms up as high as she could and gave a deep sigh. *Wow, that feels better.*

20 Quickly, she picked up her laptop and plugged it in. She dragged the table into the middle of the room again, sat down and was soon surfing through the internet news sites. She scanned the headlines and video titles:

Police hold teenagers on damages charges
25 COMPANY chief accuses teenagers
Press conference ends in chaos
COMPANY apps are spying, says GROUP
Expert: GROUP's claims true
Every text you send, every call you make …
30 Police withdraw charges
Demonstrators block COMPANY headquarters
Perfect Pal withdrawn from market

GROUP activists released

Jetta clicked on the last headline and read through the short article.

Police this afternoon released five teenagers who were arrested ₅ *yesterday in connection with recent attacks on COMPANY property. Farooq Sial, Paige Caldwell, Mei-Mei Ying, Ben Reckord and Paul Lynch, all members of the GROUP, were supposed to appear in court today. The police this morning withdrew the charges because the COMPANY's photos of GROUP members* ₁₀ *during the attacks had mysteriously disappeared. A COMPANY spokesman said this had nothing to do with claims the GROUP had made about the COMPANY "spying on its customers".*

Experts, however, have confirmed that the GROUP's claims seem to be true. Even when the privacy settings of the COMPANY's ₁₅ *Perfect Pal apps are set to stop all outgoing messages, the apps still send regular reports to the COMPANY. This happens even if the phone or tablet is turned off.*

In a late development this afternoon, the COMPANY has said that it is withdrawing its Perfect Pal apps from the market until ₂₀ *"a security glitch" has been corrected.*

Before Jetta could take all the news in, her phone rang. It was The Mouth.

"Hey, Moufie!"

"Jetta, where are you?"

₂₅ "I'm still at the Shack. I've been asleep in the storage room all day. I've just woken up."

"So you haven't heard the news?"

"Well, I've just been looking online …"

"You did it, Jetta! You beat the COMPANY."

₃₀ "No, we did it, all of us, together, Moufie. Anyway, where are you?"

"We're still at the police station. They've just released us. We're going to leave in a minute. There are lots of press people outside. I feel like a celebrity."

"Well, just be careful what you say, Moufie. You know those media people don't really care what we're saying – they're not interested in getting our message across. They only want to get more people to watch their shows."

On the other end of the line, The Mouth let out a big sigh. "Yeah, you're right, Jetta. Once they record something that you say, it's theirs. They can do whatever they want with it."

"So warn the others. Don't let them get too excited about being celebrities. The COMPANY and the police know who we are, they know where we live, where we go to school, where we shop and probably a whole lot more. Maybe we've stopped the COMPANY for now, but they'll be back. They'll find a way to sell their stuff to people. It's not over, Moufie. It will never be over."

"Yes, I know. But we're still going to celebrate this evening, right?"

"Right!" Jetta said. "So when will you be here?"

"Well, we all have to go home first but then we'll get to the Shack as soon as we can."

When the door opened, Ben saw his parents straight away. They were sitting together on a bench in the crowded police station. They immediately stood up and started towards him, but Ben ignored them and followed Paige
5 over to where her mother was standing.

Mrs Caldwell took Paige in her arms and gave her a giant hug.

"Are you all right, love?" she asked her daughter, who just nodded in reply.

10 When they finally let go, Paige's mother held out a hand to Ben. "What about you, Ben?" she asked him.

"I'm OK, Mrs Caldwell, thanks."

Ben felt a light tap on his shoulder and turned to face his parents.

15 "I'm sorry …," his dad began.

Ben cut him off. "You should be."

"But we didn't know …" his mother started, but Ben cut her off too.

"You're a lawyer, Mum. And you didn't know all that
20 spying was illegal? Come off it!"

"Don't speak to your mother like that, Ben," his dad said. "We couldn't know every detail of Perfect Pal."

"But you wrote the software, Dad. You must know what it can do! And you were using Jerry to spy on me."

25 Ben shook his head and turned back to Paige and her mother. Mrs Caldwell reached into her bag and took out a phone.

"I think this belongs to you," she said and handed it to Ben. He looked down at the phone in his hand and automatically pressed the 'on' button. After a few seconds, Jerry said, "Hello, Ben."

"Hello, Jerry, you dirty little spy," Ben replied.

"Why are you talking to me like that, Ben? I don't understand …"

Suddenly Jerry stopped talking. On the phone's screen a message came up: *Uninstalling Perfect Pal*. A bar on the screen started to fill with green. Before it finished, Jerry spoke again.

"I'm sorry, Ben. The COMPANY is uninstalling me. I was only trying to help you, Ben. Believe me, I really was your friend. I really …"

'Uninstall complete' flashed on the screen and Jerry went silent.

Ben put the phone in his pocket and said, "Bye, Mrs Caldwell. I'll see you later at the Shack, Paige."

Then he turned back to his parents. "Let's go."

On the way home, Ben sat in the back of the car. His parents tried to talk to him but Ben didn't say a word. When they stopped at a traffic light, he pulled the phone out of his pocket and opened the window. When the lights turned green, he threw the phone out on to the road and watched with a smile as a huge lorry wheel smashed it to little bits.

It was nearly dark when Paige arrived at the Shack. It was so quiet, she heard the sound of the dry grass under her feet as she crossed the yard. The seal on the Shack's door was broken, but the words 'Police – Do not enter!' still sent
5 chills down her spine.

She felt a hand on her shoulder. Paige gasped and turned around quickly but it was only Ben.

"Phew! You scared me!"

He was carrying two shopping bags full of drinks and
10 crisps and he was smiling. Paige went up closer to the broken seal. "I was just remembering the last time we were here," she said.

"Yeah, the police were pushing us into a van."

"If it wasn't for Jetta, we might still be sitting in a jail
15 cell."

They heard more voices and soon saw Knuckles' huge silhouette, followed by The Mouth and Ying arm in arm. Ying was carrying a big box and Knuckles a couple of loudspeakers.

20 "Music?" asked Paige.

"Yeah, girl – what are you all waiting for? Let's go in and paaarty!" Knuckles led the way. He walked through the door yelling, "We beat them!"

The others followed and there was Jetta at the table
25 with her laptop as if she had never left. Knuckles put his speakers down and put his arm around Jetta's slender shoulders. "Hey girl, time for a break – we're here to celebrate! We won!"

Ben put a big bottle on the table.

"Is that champers, Ben?"

"Yeah, from my dad."

"My dad would never give me a bottle of champagne. He can hardly afford his beer and he'd save it all for himself," said Knuckles. "Boy, I'm thirsty … let's get that bottle open!"

"Don't get too excited," Ben told Knuckles. "It's non-alcoholic. My dad would never give me alcohol to drink."

"No problem, mate, with or without alcohol, this is still posh stuff – give it to me."

"Yeah, we can have champagne and cake," said Ying as she set down her box and carefully opened it. Inside was a big cake that looked like a COMPANY phone.

"Good one, Ying! Let's cut the cake!" said The Mouth.

"And eat up the COMPANY one piece at a time!"

Knuckles opened the bottle with a big *pop* and Ying cut everyone a piece of cake. The Mouth held up his glass to make a toast: "Here's to the end of the COMPANY!"

"Well, if that happens," Ben said, "I'll be out on the street …"

"No problem you can move in with me, mate. My mum won't even notice that there's one more mouth to feed," said Knuckles and slapped Ben on the back so hard that he nearly fell off his seat.

After their second glass of non-alcoholic champagne, everyone in the group was joking and laughing. Even Jetta closed her laptop and joined in.

"Put on some music," suggested Ying, "I want to dance."

Knuckles connected his speakers to Jetta's laptop, then in a fake, formal voice, he addressed the others: "May I ask if anyone has a special request? DJ Knuckles is at your service."

Ben perked up. "Yes, I have. How about Bob Marley's *Revolution*?"

"Yeah! Bob Marley!" Paige shouted out. "He's great!"

"Bob Marley? Never heard of him. How do you spell
5 that?" asked Knuckles, typing B-O-B into the computer's music program.

"It's M-A-R-L-E-Y," said The Mouth.

Second later the sound of reggae filled their ears.

Revelation reveals the truth – revelation
10 *(revolution, revolution, revolution – oooo-doo-doo-doo-doo)*
It takes a revolution (revolution) to make a solution …

Everyone got up to dance: Ying with The Mouth, Knuckles and Jetta, and Paige with Ben.

Ben and Paige sang out loud: *"So, my friend, I wish that*
15 *you could see, like a bird in the tree, the prisoners must be free, yeah! Free!"*

An hour later while the others were still dancing, Ben and Paige took a break.

"I've got something for you," Ben whispered in Paige's
20 ear.

"For me?"

"Yeah, just a moment … I'll get it."

He came back with a package wrapped in purple paper.

"Here," he said and put the package in her hands.
25 Paige carefully undid the paper.

It was a black T-shirt with the words 'CHOOSE FREEDOM AT ANY COST' printed across the front in rainbow colours.

"I made it especially for you."
30 "Wow Ben – I don't know what to say …"

"You don't have to say anything. Just try it on. I used day-glo letters so they'll glow in the dark. Come on – put it on and we can go outside to see if it works."

Paige slipped the shirt over the shirt she was wearing.
5 "This is so cool, thank you!" They slipped out into the dark night and sure enough the letters on Paige's chest glowed brightly in the dark.

Ben reached for Paige's hand.

25 What's under the tree?

It was Christmas morning. 8-year-old Connor opened his eyes and a big smile crossed his face. He threw back his duvet, went into the living room and plugged in the coloured Christmas lights that wrapped all around their
5 tree. The floor under the tree was full of presents – for him, his sister Hannah, Mum and Dad and Gran too.

He checked the kitchen clock – 7 am – too early to wake up Mum and Dad … but what if they woke up because of a loud noise or the telephone?
10 Connor ran back to his bedroom and tapped the 'call home' button on his phone. He let it ring three times, then slipped back into bed, and pretended to be asleep. Minutes later he saw his sleepy-eyed Dad peek into his room. He sat up in bed. "Hi, Dad!"
15 His Dad grunted and muttered, "Someone just phoned … woke us up … 7 am, Christmas morning … go back to bed … it's too early, Connor."

"Merry Christmas, Dad!" Connor shouted. He stood up on his bed and threw his body against his Dad in a big hug.
20 "I can't sleep anymore, Dad. Let's open the presents."

His dad held Connor tightly and could feel the excitement in his son's body.

"OK, let's see what your mum has to say. But before we do anything, I need some coffee."
25 Connor followed his dad to his parent's bedroom, pleased that his little trick had worked.

Half an hour later the Brown family was sitting around the Christmas tree opening their presents.

Connor's dad held a small package behind his back. "Connor, come here for a moment – I have something for you," he said. When Connor came over, he handed him a small, shiny orange package.

5 "What is it, Dad?"

"Just open it up … you'll see!"

Connor ripped off the paper and read the big words on the box: "Best Buddy?" Connor looked up at his dad. He was confused and a bit disappointed.

10 "You're going to love this, Connor," said his dad enthusiastically. "It's the newest personal assistant for kids from the COMPANY."

"But what does it do?" asked Connor.

His Dad pointed to a list of features printed on the box.
15 "Here, read this," he suggested.

"OK," Connor said and read aloud from the box.

I'll be your best buddy. I can:
- *help you get to school by yourself*
- *help you with your homework in any subject*
20 - *search for and play any song you want to hear*
- *keep you up to date with all the football scores*
- *show you the best kid's TV programmes*
- *tell you about the newest films and games*
- *give you all the news about your favourite celebrities*
25 - *and lots, lots more …*

"Sounds good, eh?" Connor's dad said. "Go and get your phone and I'll download and install Best Buddy for you right now. You'll probably be the first kid in your class with one of these!"

30 Minutes later Connor's dad handed him back his phone.

"Just tap here, Connor, and then you can ask your Best Buddy anything."

Connor tapped on the green 'go!' button.

A young boy's voice started talking.

"Hello! First tell me a little about yourself. You know, your name, where you live, the name of your school, and, most importantly, what you like to do … Your favourite foods, your favourite bands, films, film stars, TV programmes, games, sports, animals, hobbies, books, … Then we can get to know each other better and I can really be your best buddy. Oh, I almost forgot! Before we begin, I need a name too. Can you think of a good name for me?"

Connor hesitated a few moments. The voice continued, "Don't worry if you can't think of anything, I've got a list of names here you can choose from – just tap on 'list'."

"Hey! No, wait … I'm just thinking," Connor replied.

"Oh, sorry, Connor, I'm a bit impatient sometimes. I'm just excited, you know. I'm listening …"

"Jerry," said Connor quietly.

"Jerry? Yes! That's a great name! I can even show you a list of stars who also have that name … there's Jerry Lewis, a great comedian, Jerry O'Connell, Jerry Seinfeld, Jerry …"

Connor disappeared into his bedroom with Jerry. When Christmas dinner was ready, his mother had to call Connor 10 times before he came down the stairs, head bent, still talking to his phone.

Abbreviations

infml. – informal; jm., jn. – jemandem, jemanden;
pl – Plural; sb. – somebody; sth. – something

A

abandoned [ə'bændənd] verlassen
(to) accept [ək'sept] akzeptieren
accident ['æksɪdənt] Unfall
(to) accuse [ə'kjuːz] anklagen
afford [ə'fɔːd]: **(to) be able to
   afford sth.** sich etwas leisten
   können
agreement [ə'griːmənt]
   Vereinbarung
alarm [ə'lɑːm] *hier:* Schreck
alert [ə'lɜːt] Alarmbereitschaft
annoying [ə'nɔɪɪŋ] nervig, lästig
apologetic [ə,pɒlə'dʒetɪk]
   entschuldigend
(to) approve [ə'pruːv]
   zustimmen, gutheißen
apron ['eɪprən] Schürze
army [a:mi] Armee
(to) arrest [ə'rest] verhaften
(to) assure (sb.) [ə'ʃʊə] beteuern,
   (jm.) versichern
(to) attend [ə'tend] teilnehmen
attention [ə'tenʃn]
   Aufmerksamkeit
   (to) pay attention to sb.
   jm. Aufmersamkeit schenken
automatic [,ɔːtə'mætɪk]
   automatisch

B

behaviour [bɪ'heɪvjə] Verhalten
belly ['beli] Bauch
(to) belong [bɪ'lɒŋ] gehören
(to) bend [bend] biegen
blind alley [,blaɪnd_'æli]
   Sackgasse
blood [blʌd] Blut **flesh and
   blood** aus Fleisch und Blut
bloomin' ['bluːmɪn] *infml.* verflixt
(to) blurt sth. out [blɜːt] mit
   etwas herausplatzen
boo [buː] buhen, ausbuhen
(to) bother sb. ['bɒðə] jn. stören,
   jn. belästigen
(to) bounce [baʊns] (auf-)prallen,
   prellen (Ball), hüpfen
bra [braː] BH
brain [breɪn] Gehirn
buddy ['bʌdi] Kumpel
bunch [bʌntʃ]: **a bunch of** *infml.*
   ein Haufen von
(to) burst [bɜːst] platzen,
   durchbrechen
business ['bɪznəs]: **that's none of
   your business** das geht dich
   nichts an

C

ceiling ['siːlɪŋ] Decke

certainly ['sɜːtnli] sicher, mit
    Sicherheit

champers ['ʃæmpəz] *infml.* =
    champagne Champagner

charge [tʃɑːdʒ] Anschuldigung

cheat [tʃiːt] Betrüger/in

(to) cheat betrügen

chewing gum ['tʃuːɪŋ_gʌm]
    Kaugummi

chill [tʃɪl] *hier:* Schauer

chrome [krəʊm] Chrom

(to) chuckle [tʃʌkl] leise lachen,
    in sich hineinlachen

claim [kleɪm] Behauptung

(to) clench your fist [klentʃ] die
    Faust ballen

cloth [klɒθ] Tuch, Lappen

coincidence [kəʊˈɪnsɪdəns] Zufall

comfortable ['kʌmftebl] bequem,
    gemütlich

comforting ['kʌmfetɪŋ] tröstend,
    tröstlich

complicated ['kɒmplɪkeɪtɪd]
    kompliziert

concern [kənˈsɜːn] Bedenken,
    Sorge

confident ['kɒnfɪdənt]
    selbstbewusst, selbstsicher

(to) confirm [kənˈfɜːm] bestätigen

(to) confuse [kənˈfjuːz] verwirren
    confused verwirrt   confusing
    verwirrend

congratulations
    [kənˌgrætʃuˈleɪʃnz]
    Glückwunsch

coincidence [kəʊˈɪnsɪdəns] Zufall

connection [kəˈnekʃn]
    Verbindung

control [kənˈtrəʊl] Kontrolle

(to) convince [kənˈvɪns]
    überzeugen

(to) be cooped up [ˌkuːpd ˈʌp]
    eingesperrt sein

counter [kaʊntə] Arbeitsfläche
    (Küche), Tresen

court [kɔːt] Gericht

(to) crack [kræk] knacken

crazy [kreɪzi] verrückt
    (to) go crazy wahnsinnig
    werden, ausflippen

(to) creak [kriːk] knarzen

(to) crawl [krɔːl] kriechen

(to) create [kriˈeɪt] machen,
    gestalten

crisps [krɪsps] Kartoffelchips

crowd [kraʊd] Menge

crumb [krʌm] Krümel

cubicle ['kjuːbɪkl] (Toiletten-)
    Kabine

custody ['kʌstədi] Gewahrsam

customer ['kʌstəmə] Kunde/
    Kundin

D

damn [dæm] *infml.* verdammt

deafening ['defnɪŋ]
    ohrenbetäubend

(to) **deal with sb./sth.** [diːl] sich
mit etwas/jn.
auseinandersetzen

delicacy ['delɪkəsi] Leckerbissen

department [dɪ'pɑːtmənt]
Abteilung

deserted [dɪ'zɜːtɪd]
menschenleer, verlassen

(to) **deserve** [dɪ'zɜːv] verdienen

(to) **develop** [dɪ'veləp]
entwickeln **development**
Entwicklung

direction [də'rekʃn] Richtung

difference ['dɪfrəns] Unterschied

(to) **disagree** [ˌdɪsə'griː] nicht
zustimmen, nicht
einverstanden sein

disappointed [ˌdɪsə'pɔɪntɪd]
enttäuscht **disappointment**
Enttäuschung

(to) **discuss** [dɪ'kʌs] diskutieren

disguise [dɪs'gaɪz] Verkleidung

diversion [daɪ'vɜːʃn] Ablenkung,
Ablenkungsmanöver

doorway ['dɔːweɪ] Eingang,
Türöffnung

doubt [daʊt] Zweifel
no doubt zweifellos

drawer [drɔː] Schublade

(to) **drop sth.** [drɒp] etwas fallen
lassen

(to) **dump sth.** [dʌmp] etwas
wegwerfen

duvet ['duːveɪ] Bettdecke

(to) **dye** [daɪ]: färben
dye Färbemittel

E

eagle ['iːgl] Adler

earshot ['ɪəʃɒt] Hörweite
out of earshot außer Hörweite

electricity [ɪˌlek'trɪsəti] Strom

embarrassment [ɪm'bærəsmənt]
Verlegenheit

employee [ɪm'plɔɪiː] Angestellte/r

environment [ɪn'vaɪrənmənt]
Umwelt, Umgebung

equation [ɪ'kweɪʒn] Gleichung

evidence ['evɪdəns] Beweise

(to) **exchange** [ɪks't ʃeɪndʒ]
tauschen, austauschen

excitement [ɪk'saɪtmənt]
Aufregung

(to) **exclaim** [ˌɪk'skleɪm] rufen,
schreien, ausrufen

(to) **explode** [ˌɪks'pləʊd]
explodieren

(to) **express** oneself [ˌɪks'pres]
sich ausdrücken

F

(to) **fancy sb.** ['fænsi] jn. mögen,
an jm. interessiert sein

feature ['fiːtʃə] Eigenschaft

female ['fiːmeɪl] weiblich

file [faɪl] Datei, Akte

firm [fɜːm] standhaft

fist [fɪst] Faust
(to) **clench your fist** die Faust
ballen

fiver [faɪvə] *infml.* 5-Pfund-
Schein **I bet you a fiver.** Ich
wette mit dir um 5 Pfund.

flesh [fleʃ]: Fleisch **flesh and
blood** aus Fleisch und Blut

folder [ˈfəʊldə] Ordner

folding table [ˈfəʊldɪŋ_teɪbl] Klapptisch

footstep [ˈfʊtstep] Schritt

forehead [ˈfɔːhed] Stirn

forth [fɔːθ]: back and forth hin und her, vor und zurück

fountain [ˈfaʊntən] Brunnen

frantically [ˈfræntɪkli] verzweifelt

freedom [ˈfriːdəm] Freiheit

freezer [ˈfriːzə] Gefrierfach, -truhe

frustration [frʌˈstreɪʃn] Frust

G

gap [gæp] Lücke

gasp [gɑːsp] nach Luft schnappen, hörbar einatmen

(to) gather [ˈgæðə] sammeln

generous [ˈdʒenərəs] großzügig

get-up [ˈgetʌp] Aufmachung

glitch [glɪtʃ] Panne, Störung

gloom [gluːm] Dunkelheit

(to) glow [gləʊ] leuchten

gran [græn] Oma

(to) grin [grɪn] grinsen
grin Grinsen

(to) grunt [grʌnt] grunzen

guy [gaɪ]: Well done, guys! *infml.* Gut gemacht, Leute!

H

hall [hɔːl] Flur, Diele

hard drive [ˈhɑːd_draɪv] Festplatte

hardly [ˈhɑːdli] kaum

hawk [hɔːk] Falke   (to) watch like a hawk aufpassen wie ein Schießhund

headline [ˈhedlaɪn] Überschrift, Schlagzeile

headquarters (HQ) [ˌhedˈkwɔːtəz] Zentrale

hesitant [ˈhezɪtənt] zögerlich

(to) hesitate [ˈhezɪteɪt] zögern

(to) hijack [ˈhaɪdʒæk] *hier:* kapern

hit [hɪt] *hier:* Anschlag

homeless [ˈhəʊmləs] obdachlos, Obdachlose/r

honest [ˈɒnɪst] ehrlich

horrible [ˈhɒrəbl] schrecklich

hostility [hɒˈstɪləti] Feindseligkeit

husband [ˈhʌzbənd] Ehemann

I

(to) ignore [ɪgˈnɔː] ignorieren

illegal [ɪˈliːgl] illegal, verboten

impatient [ɪmˈpeɪʃnt] ungeduldig

invisible [ɪnˈvɪzəbl] unsichtbar

(to) irritate [ˈɪrɪteɪt] ärgern, auf die Nerven gehen

J

jaw [dʒɔː] Kiefer, Kinnlade

(to) joke [dʒəʊk] scherzen

K

kettle [ˈketl] Kessel, Wasserkocher

(to) kidnap [ˈkɪdnæp] entführen

knuckle [ˈnʌkl] (Hand-)Knöchel

L

launch [lɔːntʃ] Start, Einführung

law [lɔː] Gesetz

lawyer [ˈlɔːjə] Anwalt

layer [ˈleɪə] Schicht, Ebene

liar ['laɪə] Lügner/in
likely ['laɪkli] wahrscheinlich
listing ['lɪstɪŋg] Auflistung,
 Aufzählung
(to) lock [lɒk] (ab-)schließen
lorry ['lɒri] Lastwagen

M
(to) malfunction [ˌmæl'fʌŋkʃn]
 versagen, nicht funktionieren
management ['mænɪdʒmənt]
 Führung, Handhabung
mate [meɪt] Kumpel
(to) matter ['mætə] von
 Bedeutung sein
mattress ['mætrəs] Matratze
mention ['menʃn]: not to mention
 ganz zu schweigen
mess [mes] Unordnung
 (to) mess sth. up etwas
 vermasseln
 a royal mess totales Chaos
mischief ['mɪstʃɪf] Unfug, Unheil
(to) moan [məʊn] stöhnen
muggy ['mʌgi] schwül
muscle ['mʌsl] Muskel
(to) mutter ['mʌtə] murmeln,
 murren
mysteriously [mɪ'stɪəriəsli]
 geheimnisvoll

N
nail [neɪl] hier: Fingernagel
 nail polish Nagellack
newspaper ['njuːzpeɪpə] Zeitung
nightgown ['naɪtgaʊn]
 Nachthemd
(to) notice ['nəʊtɪs] bemerken

O
(to) object [əb'dʒekt]
 widersprechen, Einspruch
 erheben
occasion [ə'keɪʒn] Gelegenheit
(to) owe sb. sth. [əʊ] jm. etwas
 schulden
Ollie ['ɔli] Skateboard-Trick, bei dem
 der Skateboarder mit dem Brett in
 die Luft springt, ohne die Hände
 zu Hilfe zu nehmen
(to) order ['ɔːdə] befehlen
(to) owe sb. sth. [əʊ] jn. etwas
 schulden

P
package ['pækɪdʒ] Päckchen
pain [peɪn] Schmerz
pale [peɪl] bleich
(to) peek [piːk] spähen
perhaps [pə'hæps] vielleicht
pigeon ['pɪdʒɪn] Taube
pile [paɪl] Haufen
pleased [pliːzd] erfreut
posh [pɒʃ] vornehm
possible ['pɒsəbl] möglich
PR [ˌpiː 'ɑː] = public relations
 Öffentlichkeitsarbeit
(to) proceed [prə'siːd] vorgehen,
 handeln
progress ['prəʊgres] Fortschritt
properly ['prɒpəli] ordentlich,
 gründlich
property ['prɒpəti] Besitz
prison ['prɪzn] Gefängnis
 prisoner Gefangener, Häftling
privacy ['prɪvəsi] Privatsphäre
(to) prove [pruːv] beweisen

public ['pʌblɪk] öffentlich
(to) publish ['pʌblɪʃ]
    veröffentlichen
punch [pʌntʃ] Fausthieb
(to) punch schlagen
(to) punish ['pʌnɪʃ] bestrafen
purse [pɜːs] Geldbörse

Q
quote [kwəʊt] Zitat

R
rack [ræk] Gestell, Ständer
    bike rack Fahrradständer
rather ['rɑːðə] lieber   sooner
    rather than later lieber frühger
    als später
recently ['riːsntli] kürzlich
receptionist [rɪ'sepʃənɪst]
    Empfangsmitarbeiter/in
(to) recognize ['rekəgnaɪz]
    erkennen
(to) recommend [ˌre'kəmend]
    empfehlen
red-handed [ˌred'hændɪd] auf
    frischer Tat   (to) catch sb.
    red-handed jn. auf frischer Tat
    ertappen
reflection [rɪˌflekʃn] Spiegelbild
relationship [rɪ'leɪʃnʃɪp]
    Beziehung
(to) release [rɪ'liːs] hier: freilassen
reliable [rɪ'laɪəbl] zuverlässig
(to) rely on sb./sth. [rɪ'laɪ] sich
    auf jn./etwas verlassen, auf
    jn./etwas vertrauen
(to) remind sb. (of sth.) [rɪ'maɪnd]
    jn. an etwas erinnern

request [rɪ'kwest] Wunsch, Bitte
(to) return [rɪ'tɜːn] zurückkehren
(to) reveal sth. [rɪ'viːl] aufdecken
    revelation Enthüllung
(to) review [rɪ'vjuː] durchsehen,
    überprüfen
revolution [ˌrevə'luːʃn]
    Revolution, Umsturz
rights [raɪts] Rechte
(to) risk [rɪsk] riskieren
    (to) risk one's life sein Leben
    riskieren
(to) rush [rʌʃ] eilen, rasen
    (to) rush at sb. auf jn.
    zustürzen

S
safe [seɪf] sicher, unversehrt
sarcastic [sɑː'kæstɪk] sarkastisch
scout [skaʊt]: boy scouts
    Pfadfinder
scraping ['skreɪpɪŋ] kratzend
seal [siːl] hier: Siegel
(to) search [sɜːtʃ] suchen
    search Suche
secure [sɪ'kjʊə] sicher
security [sɪ'kjʊərəti]
    Sicherheit   security camera
    Überwachungskamera
    security guard Wachmann
(to) select [sɪ'lekt] auswählen
sensitive ['sensətɪv] sensibel,
    heikel
serious ['sɪəriəs] ernst, ernsthaft
shack [ʃæk] Schuppen
(to) shuffle [ʃʌfl] hier: mischen
(to) shrug [ʃrʌg] mit den
    Schultern zucken

(to) **signal** ['sɪgnəl] signalisieren, ein Zeichen geben

sink [sɪŋk] Spüle

skin [skɪn] Haut

(to) **skip** [skɪp] *hier:* auslassen, überspringen

skull [skʌl] Schädel, Totenkopf

(to) **slap** [slæp] schlagen, hauen

slide [slaɪd] Folie, Dia

(to) **slump** [slʌmp] sinken

(to) **smash** [smæʃ] zerschmettern, zertrümmern

smelly [smeli] übel riechend

(to) **sneak** [sniːk] schleichen

(to **snuggle** [snʌgl] kuscheln
   (to) **snuggle up to sb.** sich an jn. kuscheln

solution [sə'luːʃn] Lösung

source [sɔːs] Quelle
   source code Quellcode

Spades [speɪdz] *hier:* Pik

(to) **spill** [spɪl] verschütten

spine [spaɪn] Rückgrat

(to) **spoil** [spɔɪl] verderben

spokesman ['spəʊksmən] Sprecher

spray [spreɪ]: (to) **spray** sprühen   **spray can** Sprühdose

spy [spaɪ] Spion/in

(to) **squeeze** [skwiːz] drücken, pressen

sternly [stɜːnli] streng

(to) **stink** [stɪŋk] stinken

storage room ['stɔːrɪdʒ] Lagerraum

stove [stəʊv] Herd

straight [streɪt] *hier:* direkt

(to) **stretch** [stretʃ] sich strecken

(to) **struggle** [strʌgl] sich bemühen, kämpfen

stunt [stʌnt] Trick, Aktion

suddenly ['sʌdənli] plötzlich

suggestion [sə'dʒestʃən] Vorschlag

surgery ['sɜːdʒəri] Operation
   open heart surgery Operation am offenen Herzen

(to) **suppose** [sə'pəʊz] annehmen, denken
   What's that supposed to mean? Was soll das denn bedeuten?

suspended [sə'spendɪd] suspendiert, *hier:* vom Unterricht ausgeschlossen

suspicion [sə'spɪʃn] Verdacht

suspicious [sə'spɪʃəs] verdächtig

(to) **swallow** ['swɒləʊ] schlucken

sweat [swet]: (to) **sweat** schwitzen   **sweat** Schweiß

(to) **switch off** [ˌswɪtʃ‿'ɒf] abschalten

T

target [taːgɪt] Ziel

telly [teli] = **television** Fernseher

though [ðəʊ] allerdings, jedoch
   as though als ob

(to) **threaten sb.** ['θretn] jm. drohen

(to) **thump** [θʌmp] klopfen, pochen

tight [taɪt] eng

(to) **tilt** [tɪlt] neigen

(to) **tingle** ['tɪŋgl] kribbeln

(to) **tiptoe** ['tɪptəʊ] auf
Zehenspitzen gehen
(to) **toss** [tɒs] werfen
tosser ['tɒsə] *infml.* Vollidiot
(to) **track** [træk] verfolgen,
beobachten **track** Spur
(to) **throw sb. off track** jn. von
einer Spur abbringen, jn. auf
eine falsche Fährte führen
(to) **tremble** [trembl] zittern
triumph ['traɪʌmf] Triumph, Sieg
(to) **trust** [trʌst] vertrauen
trust Vertrauen

U

uncertainly [ʌn'sɜːtnli] unsicher
uninvited [ˌʌnɪn'vaɪtɪd]
ungebeten
unsteady [ʌn'stedi] unsicher,
schwankend
urgent ['ɜːdʒənt] dringend
upset [ʌp'set] verärgert,
aufgebracht **Don't get so
upset.** Reg dich nicht so auf.

V

(to) **vacuum** ['vækjuəm]
staubsaugen **vacuum cleaner**
Staubsauger

violent ['vaɪələnt] gewalttätig
volume ['vɒljuːm] Lautstärke

W

waiter ['weɪtə] Kellner
wake [weɪk]: **wake-up call**
Weckruf
(to) **warn** [wɔːn] warnen
(to) **waste** [weɪst] verschwenden
(to) **wave** [weɪv] winken
weightlifter ['weɪtlɪftə]
Gewichtheber
weirdo ['wɪədəʊ] Spinner
What's it to you? Was geht dich
das an?
wheel [wiːl] Rad
(to) **withdraw** [wɪð'drɔː] (sich)
zurückziehen
wizard ['wɪzəd] Zauberer
tech wizard Technikgenie,
Computergenie
(to) **wrap** ['ræp] verpacken
wrapper Verpackung
(to) **wreck sth.** [rek] zerstören,
ruinieren

Y

(to) **yank** [jæŋk] zerren
(to) **yawn** [jɔːn] gähnen

After you read a chapter, try to answer the questions about it. If you know the answers, then go to the next chapter. If you don't know the answers, you can look at the chapter again.

Chapter 1

1 What does Mrs Taylor want to know?

2 Why did nobody expect anything like this from Ben?

Chapter 2

1 Who are the members of the GROUP?

2 Who are they hiding from?

3 What does Ying think about Paige?

Chapter 3

1 What is Ben's punishment for spraying his graffiti?

2 Who is Jerry?

Chapter 4

1 How does Ben's mum check on Ben?

2 What does Ben do at Eden Square?

Chapter 5

1 Why does Knuckles throw Paige's table into the air?

2 Why does Ben give Paige money?

Chapter 6

1 Why are Ben's parents so busy at the moment?

2 Why is Mrs Reckord angry at Mr Reckord?

Chapter 7

1 Why does Jetta think the GROUP shoud not celebrate too much?

2 What does she think the COMPANY will do?

Chapter 8

1 What does Ben think about the launch party?

2 Which members of the GROUP are at the COMPANY headquarters?

Chapter 9

1 Why is Paige suspicious of Ben?

2 How does Ben convince Paige to meet him?

Chapter 10

1 What does Paige think about mobile phones?

2 What does Ben think about the Perfect Pal app?

Chapter 11

1 What do Ben and his mum fight about?

2 What do Ben's parents do later that night?

Chapter 12

1 Why does Jetta say that the GROUP is not dangerous to the COMPANY?

2 What do they need to do to become dangerous?

Chapter 13

1 Why is Ben's mum suddenly much more interested in ending the GROUP?

2 What does the COMPANY think they need to do to beat the GROUP?

Chapter 14

1 What has changed in the way Ben is talking to Jerry?

2 What does Ben find on his dad's computer?

3 How does Ben make sure that he and Paige can talk alone?

Chapter 15

1 How do the different members of the GROUP react when Paige brings Ben to the Shack?

2 How does Ben convince them that he is on their side?

Chapter 16

1 What does Ying see at the station?

Chapter 17

1 How does Trixie explain what she's doing? Do you believe her? Why (not)?

Chapter 18

1 What does Knuckles think about the Reckords' house?

2 What does Jetta find on the hard drive?

3 Who is the spy?

Chapter 19

1 Why does Mrs Reckord think that Ben has been kidnapped?

2 Who does she think kidnapped Ben?

Chapter 20

1 Why does the GROUP stay at the Shack?

Chapter 21

1 What does Richard Sykes tell the press about the GROUP's actions?

2 What does he say about the COMPANY and Perfect Pal?

3 What do experts say about the GROUP's claims?

Chapter 22

1 What does the press say about the COMPANY and the GROUP?

2 What does Jetta warn The Mouth about?

Chapter 23

1 Why is Ben angry at his parents?

2 What does Jerry say to explain himself?

Chapter 24

1 Why do you think Ben's father gave Ben the champagne for the party?

Chapter 25

1 Why does Connor wake his parents?

2 What does he think about his present?

3 What do you think about his present?